# THE SHAKESPEARE ASSOCIATION FACSIMILES

## No. 1

# THE SHAKESPEARE ASSOCIATION FACSIMILES

A series of rare texts illustrating life and thought in Shakespeare's England, under the general editorship of Dr. G. B. Harrison. The first four volumes:—

(1) *A Dialogue Concerning Witches and Witchcraftes.* By GEORGE GIFFORD. 1593. With an Introduction by BEATRICE WHITE.

(2) *Skialetheia; or a Shadow of Truth in Certaine Epigrams and Satyres.* By EVERARD GUILPIN. 1598.

(3) *A Health to the Gentlemanly Profession of Serving-Men.* By I.M. 1598. With an Introduction by A. V. JUDGES.

(4) *Vicissitudo Rerum.* By JOHN NORDEN. 1600. With an Introduction by D. C. COLLINS.

All four volumes are issued to Members in return for the guinea subscription for 1931. Further volumes in this series will be issued in 1932.

SHAKESPEARE ASSOCIATION
FACSIMILES NO. 1

# A Dialogue Concerning Witches and Witchcraftes

1593

*by* GEORGE GIFFORD

WITH AN INTRODUCTION BY
BEATRICE WHITE

*Published for*
THE SHAKESPEARE ASSOCIATION
*by*
Humphrey Milford, Oxford University Press
Amen House, Warwick Square, E.C.
1931

# INTRODUCTION

IN contradistinction to the scientific demonology of France and Germany, English witchcraft of the sixteenth century was a flat, dull, vulgar, unimaginative affair. Perhaps as a consequence the annals of English witchcraft are not so dark and terrible as they might easily have been. Although there exist details of over two hundred cases of witchcraft between the years 1563 and 1603, the prosecution of witches in England was not marked by the insane ferocity that burnt nine hundred witches in the province of Lorraine alone between 1580 and 1595, according to Remigius, and in 1524 put to death one thousand unfortunate wretches in Como according to de Spina.

In England popular ideas on witchcraft had none of the fine exuberance of the Scottish witch cult or the wild imagination of the cult as it revealed itself on the Continent. Gifford's work admirably exemplifies the unimaginative character of the popular witchcraft creed of the Elizabethan period. There were no sabbaths, no unholy sacraments and hideous feasts, no airy excursions to distant Blockulas, no abominable lycanthropy, no voyages to sea in sieves, no journeys to Elfland, no direct liaison with the devil. Gifford's witches are just bad-tempered old women with a grudge against individuals or the world at large and the victims of their own spite. They have their imps or "puckrels," familiar spirits in the shape of cats, toads, weasels, and other vermin, and these they send forth to kill men and cattle, rewarding them with food and keeping them in pots of wool under their beds. One old lady with more imagination keeps her spirit in a hollow tree. Gifford is remarkable for his tolerance, humanity, and occasional good sense. Never for a moment does he doubt the existence of witches. With him, as with Scot, it is not a question of *de existentia* but of *de modo existendi*. He regards witchcraft as a horrible machination of the devil to bring both accusers and accused to destruction. The devil is the Lord's executioner. His book is valuable because it is compiled not from foreign authorities like the *Malleus Malificarum* and the work of Wierus, but from honest observation of local gossip and an attendance on the witch trials of the time.

In the sixteenth century witchcraft was not a mere subject for speculation; conjuration and murder by witchcraft carried the death penalty and were constantly punished at the assizes. The supernatural held sway over the minds of men in every rank of life, from the noble earl to the miserable cottager, from the learned Dr. Dee to the ordinary village "cunning man." Men of education were reading the *Malleus Malificarum*, Nider's *Formicarum*, Wierus, and Bodin. In 1572 Lavater's *De Spectris* was translated into English, and in 1575 the work of Danæus on witches. Witch trials were frequent and aroused much curiosity and excitement. In Scotland, in 1576, Bessie Dunlop's weird story of her familiar Thome Reid brought about her death. In 1588 Alison Peirsoun, who made a most extraordinary confession, was tried and condemned, and 1590 was remarkable for the trials of Lady Fowlis and Hector Munro, and for the famous trial of the North Berwick witches who attempted to murder James VI. In England, in Essex alone, three witches were put to death at Chelmsford in 1579, and at St. Osyth's in 1582 thirteen or eighteen witches were discovered and destroyed. In 1589 three more witches were condemned at Chelmsford, and in 1593 the unfortunate Samwells of Warboys were executed for bewitching to death the Lady Cromwell. The St. Osyth's trials possibly induced Scot to write *The Discoverie of Witchcraft* in 1584. It seems more than probable that Gifford, minister of God's word at Maldon, Essex, in the midst of a superstitious district famous in the history of witchcraft, attended these trials and others in the neighbourhood. He clearly perceived the inadequacy of the evidence on which convictions were made, and in 1587 he produced his first work on witchcraft, *A Discourse of the subtill Practises of Deuilles by Witches and Sorcerers*. In this he defines a witch as "one that woorketh by the Deuill, or by some deuilish or curious art, either hurting or healing, reuealing thinges secrete or foretelling thinges to come, which the deuil hath deuised to entangle and snare mens soules withal vnto damnation. The coniurer, the enchaunter, the sorcerer, the deuiner, and whatsoeuer other sort there is, are in deede compassed within this circle."

It is obvious that the witches of *Macbeth* are very far removed from the common or garden English witch with her imps in pots of wool under her bed. They have romantic Scottish and Continental features. They are "weird sisters" and they are at the same time "secret, black and mid-night hags." They are awe-inspiring embodiments of evil, yet they descend to the trivialities of killing swine and sailing the seas in a sieve to be revenged on a sailor's greedy wife; they have familiars, they fly through the air, and they raise spectres by means of a nocturnal brew of hideous and disgusting ingredients. They are Gifford's witches continentalised, and, as it were, sublimated, who yet remain of the earth, earthy. Margery Jourdain and Bolingbroke in the second part of *Henry VI* are historical figures clearly presented, and as such need no comment. Prospero, as a conjuror, certainly comes under Gifford's definition of witch, and is Dr. Dee translated to the sphere of poetry. Sycorax is the typical malignant Gifford witch. It is worth noticing that she confined Ariel in a cleft pine in much the same way, I suppose, as the old woman in the Dialogue kept her spirit in a hollow tree.

Like his contemporary, Reginald Scot, Gifford was a student at Hart Hall, Oxford, before 1568. In August, 1582, he was presented to the living of All Saints with St. Peter's at Maldon. From 1573-1590 he produced numerous theological works and won a reputation for vigorous preaching. He became a prominent Nonconformist, and in January 1584 he joined a synod of Nonconformist Essex ministers in London and publicly refused to subscribe to the articles of the Established Church. For this act he was suspended from his living and subsequently arrested. In June 1584 he was deprived of his living at Maldon, but was allowed to hold the office of lecturer and continue preaching. In 1587 he was suspended from this lectureship, but he seems to have continued his work as a leader of the Essex Nonconformists and attended synods in 1587 and 1589. In 1591 he preached at Paul's Cross, and in 1620 died at Maldon, where the reformation effected by his preaching had won him great esteem.

His two excursions into Demonology deserve to be remembered, not only for their tolerant spirit and the moderation of their views, but as compendiums of the curious superstitions of his time and for the vigorous colloquial English in which they are written.

Those who wish to pursue the subject further should consult the excellent bibliographies appended to Montague Summer's *History of Witchcraft* and *Geography of Witchcraft*, also E. Wallace Notestein's *History of Witchcraft in England from 1558-1718*, C. L'Estrange Ewen's *Witch Hunting and Witch Trials*, and Miss Margaret Alice Murray's *Witchcult in Western Europe*.

BEATRICE WHITE.

# BIBLIOGRAPHY

First edition 1593.

Second edtion 1603.

Percy Society, Vol. VIII, No. 24, reprinted from the second edition in 1842.

This facsimile is taken from the copy of the first edition in the British Museum (c. 57 e. 43) from which, however, sign B.1. is missing; it has been supplied from the Bodleian copy.

# A
# DIALOGVE
### concerning VVitches
### *and Witchcraftes.*

In which is laide open how craftely
*the Diuell deceiueth not onely the Witches*
but many other and so leadeth them
awrie into many great
*errours.*

**By** George Giffard Miniſter of Gods
*word in Maldon.*

**LONDON.**

Printed by *Iohn Windet* for Tobie Cooke and Mi-
hil Hart, and are to be ſold in Pauls Chnrch-
yard, at the Tygers head. 1593.

*Made and Printed by the Replika Process in Great Britain by
Percy Lund, Humphries & Co. Ltd.
3 Amen Corner, London, E.C.4
and at Bradford*

# TO THE RIGHT VVOR-
## SHIPFVLL MAISTER Ro-
### bert Clarke, one of her Maiesties Barons
### of her Highnes Court of Eschequer.

Ertaine yeares now past, right
Worshipfull , I published a
small Treatise concerning
Witches, to lay open some
of Sathans sleightes, and subtill practises, least the ignoran-
ter sort should be carried a-
wry and seduced more and more by them. The
errors be farre more grosse, and the sinnes much
greater, into which by meanes of Witches he sedu-
ceth multitudes, then in common opinion they be
esteemed. It falleth out in many places euen of a
suddaine, as it seemeth to me, and no doubt by the
heauy iudgement of God, that the Diuels as it were
let loose, doe more preuail, then euer I haue heard
of. For when as men haue set so light by the hea-

A 2                ring

ring of Gods voice to be inſtructed by him, they
are iuſtly giuen ouer to be taught by the Diuels,
and to learne their waies. Sathan is now hearde
ſpeake, and beleeued. He ſpeaketh by coniurors,
by ſorcerers, and by witches, and his word is taken.
He deuiſeth a number of thinges to be done, and
they are put in practiſe and followed. The high
prouidence of God Almighty and ſoueraigne rule
ouer all, is ſet forth ſo vnto vs in the Scriptures, as
that without him a Sparrow can not fall vpon the
ground. All the haires of our head are numbred.
The Deuils would hurt and deſtroy with bodily
harmes, both men and beaſtes and other creatures:
but all the Diuels in Hell are ſo chained vp and bri-
deled by this high prouidence that they can not
plucke the wing from one poore little Wrenne,
without ſpeciall leaue giuen them from the ruler
of the whole earth. And yet the Witches are made
beleeue that at their requeſt, and to pleaſure them
by fulfilling their wrath, their ſpirites doe lame and
kill both men and beaſtes. And then to ſpread this
opinion among the people, theſe ſubtill ſpirites bewray them, and will haue them openly confeſſe
that they haue done ſuch great things, which all the
Diuels at any mans requeſt cold neuer doe. For if
they could, they would not ſtay to be intreated.
God giueth him power ſometimes to afflict both
men and beaſtes with bodily harmes : If he can, he
will

will doe it, as intreated and ſent by Witches, but for vs to imagin either that their ſending doth giue him power, or that he would not doe that which God hath giuen him leaue to doe, vnleſſe they ſhould requeſt and ſend him, is moſt abſurd. There be many diſeaſes in the bodies of men and beaſtes which he ſeeth will breake forth vnto lamenes or vnto death, he beareth the witches in hand he doth them: He worketh by his other ſort of Witches, whome the people call cunning men and wiſe women to confirme all his matters, and by them teacheth many remedies, that ſo he may be ſought vnto and honored as God. Theſe things taking root in the hearts of the people, and ſo making them afraide of Witches, and raiſing vp ſuſpitions and rumors of ſundry innocent perſons, many giltles are vppon mens othes condemned to death, and much innocent bloud is ſhed. How ſubtilly he continueth theſe matters, I haue to my ſmal skill laide open in this ſlender Treatiſe. I haue done it in waye of a Dialogue, to make the fitter for the capacity of the ſimpler ſort. I am bolde to offer it vnto your Worſhip, not vnto one as needeth to be taught in theſe thinges, being zealouſly affected to the Goſpell, & ſo grounded in the faith of the high prouidence, that I haue been delighted to heare and ſee the wiſe and godly courſe vſed vppon the ſeat of Iuſtice by your Worſhip, when ſuch haue beene arraigned. I

offer

## The Epiſtle.

offer it therefore as a teſtimony of a thankeful mind
for fauours and kindneſſe ſhewed towardes me:
and ſo intreat your Worſhippe to accept of it. If
it may doe good vnto any of the weaker ſort
in knowledge I ſhall be glad. If I erre
in any thing being ſhewed it, I will
be ready to correct it.

*Your Worſhips in all dueties
to commaund.*

George Giffard.

Samuell. Daniell. The wife of Samuell. M. B.
Schoolemaifter. The good wife R.

Sam.

Ou are well mette olde acquaintance, I am glad to
feé you looke fo well, howe
doe all our good friendes
in your Countrey.

Dan.

I truft they be all in
good health, they were
when I came from home,
I am fozry to feé you looke
fo pale, what haue you beéne ficke lately?

Sam. Truely no, I thanke God I haue had my health
pzetily well, but yet me thinke my meate doth me no good
of late.

Dan. What is the matter man, doe you take thought
and care foz the wozld : take heéde of that, foz the Scripture faith, wozldly fozrow wozketh death. 2. Cor. 7. 10.
It is a great finne rifing from vnbeleéfe, and diftruft in
Gods pzouidence, when men be ouer penfiue foz the wozld.

Sam. In deéde my minde is troubled, but not foz that
which you fay, foz I hope in God I fhall not want fo long
as I liue.

Dan. Is it any trouble of confcience foz finne? If it
be, that may turne to good.

Sam. O, no, no. I know no caufe why.

Dan. Why, what is it then, if I may be fo bold, I pzay
you

you tell me. I thinke you take me for your friend.

Sam. In deede I haue alwaies found you my very good friend, and I am sure you will giue me the best counsell you can, truely we dwell here in a bad countrey, I think euen one of the worst in England.

Dan. Is it so? I thinke you dwell in a fine countrey, in a sweete wholesome aire and fruitfull grounds.

Sam. Aire man? I finde no fault with the aire, there be naughty people.

Dan. Naughty people: where shall a man dwell, and not finde them? swearers, liars, raylers, slaunderers, drunckards, adulterers, riotous, vnthriftes, dicers, and proude high minded persons, are euery where to be founde in great plenty.

Sam. Nay, I doe not meane them, I care not for them. These witches, these euill fauoured old witches doe trouble me.

Dan. What doe you take your selfe to be bewitched?

Sam. No, no, I trust no euill spirite can hurt me, but I heare of much harme done by them: they lame men and kill their cattle, yea they destroy both men and children. They say there is scarce any towne or village in all this shire, but there is one or two witches at the least in it. In good sooth, I may tell it to you as to my friend, when I goe but into my closes, I am afraide, for I see nowe and then a Hare; which my conscience giueth me is a witch, or some witches spirite, shee stareth so vppon me. And sometime I see an vgly weasell runne through my yard, and there is a foule great catte sometimes in my Barne, which I haue no liking vnto.

Dan. You neuer had no hurt done yet, had you by any witch?

Sam. Trust me I cannot tell, but I feare me I haue,

for

for there be two or three in our towne which I like not, but especially an old woman, I haue béene as careful to please her as euer I was to please mine own mother, and to giue her euer anon one thing or other, and yet me thinkes shee frownes at me now and then. And I had a hogge which eate his meate with his fellowes and was very well to our thinking ouer night, and in the morning he was starke dead. My wife hath had fiue or sire hennes euen of late dead. Some of my neighbours wishe me to burne some thing aliue, as a henne or a hogge. Others will me in time to séeke helpe at the handes of some cunning man, before I haue any further harme. I wold be glad to do for the best.

Dan. Haue you any cunning man hereabout, that doth helpe?

Sam. There is one, they say, here a twenty miles of at T. B. which hath holpe many. And thus much I know, there was one of mine acquaintance but two miles hence, which had great losses, he lost two or thrée kine; sir hogs, he would not haue tooke fisteene shillings a hog for them, and a mare. He went to that same man, and told him hée suspected an old woman in the parish. And I think he told me, that he shewed him her in a Glasse, and tolde him shee had thrée or foure imps, some call them puckrels, one like a gray catte, an other like a weasell, an other like a mouse, a vengeance take them, it is great pitty the countrey is not ridde of them, and told him also what he shoulde doe, it is halfe a yeare agoe, and he neuer had any hurt since. There is also a woman at R. H. fiue and twenty miles hence, that hath a great name, and great resort there is dayly vnto her. A neighbour of mine had his childe taken lame, a girle of ten yeares olde, and such a paine in her backe, that shée could not sit vpright. He went to that woman, she tolde him he had some badde neighbour, the childe was forespoken, as he suspected; marry if he would goe home, and bring her som of the clothes which the child

B                                                    lay

lay in all night, shée would tell him certainely. He went home, and put a table Napkin about her necke all night, and in the morning tooke it with him, and shée told him the girle was bewitched in deede, and so told him what hee should doe, and he had remedy, the girle is as wel at this day, and a pretty quicke girle. There was another of my neighbours had his wife much troubled, and he went to her, and shée tolde him, his wife was haunted with a Fairy. I cannot tell what shée bad him doe, but the woman is merry at this howze. I haue heard, I dare not say it is so, that shée weareth about her Sainct Iohns Gospel, or some part of it.

Dan. If you haue such cunning men and women, what néede you be so much afraide?

Sam. Alas man, I could teeme it to goe, and some counsell me to goe to the man at T. B. and some to the woman at R. H. And betweene them both I haue lingred the time, and feare I may be spoiled before I get remedy. Some wishe me to beate and claw the witch vntill I fetch blood on her, and to threaten her that I will haue her hanged, if I knew which were the best I would doe it.

Dan. I perceiue your danger is betwéene two stooles.

Sam. It is very true, if I had heard but of one, I should haue gone ere this time, and I am glad that I met with you. I pray you let me haue your best counsell, I trust you beare me good will.

Dan. Truely I will giue you the best counsell I can, which I am sure shall doe you good, if you will followe it, for in deede I pitty your case, it is most certaine you are bewitched.

Sam. Bewitched, doe you thinke I am bewitched? I feele no harme in my body, you make me more afraide.

Dam. Nay I doe not thinke that the olde woman hath bewitched you, or that your body is bewitched, but the diuell hath bewitched your minde, with blindnes and vnbe-

léefe,

# witches and witchcraftes.

leſe, to draw you from God, euen to worſhip himſelfe, by ſeeking help at the hands of deuils. It is a lamentable caſe to ſee how the deuill hath bewitched thouſands at this day to run after him: and euen to offer ſacrifice vnto him.

Sam. I defie the deuill, worſhip him? fie vpon him, I hate him with all my hart. Do you thinke any ſeeke help at his hands? we ſeek help againſt him. I thinke he neuer doth good, he hurteth, but he neuer helpeth any.

Dan. It is not in theſe matters to be taken as wee imagine, but as the word of God teacheth. What though a man think he worſhippeth not deuils, nor ſeeketh not help at their handes, as he is perſuaded, nor hath any ſuch intent, is he euer the neere, when as yet it ſhall be found by Gods word, that he doth worſhip them, and ſeek vnto them for help?

Sam. Doe you thinke then that there be no witches? Doth not God ſuffer wicked people to do harme? Or doe you thinke that the cunning men doe helpe by the deuill? I would be glad to reaſon with you, but I haue ſmal knowledge in the ſcripturs. We haue a Schoolemaiſter that is a good pretie ſcholler, they ſay, in the Latine tongue, one M. B. he is gone to my houſe euen now, I pray you let me intreat you to go thither, you two may reaſon the matter, for you are learned.

Dan. I could be content, but it will aſke ſome time, and I am going to ſuch a place vpon ſpeciall buſines.

Sam. I pray you let mee intreat you: Foure or fiue houres is not ſo much.

Dan. Well, I will goe with you.

Sam. Wife, I haue brought an olde friend of mine, I pray thee bid him welcome.

The wife. He is verie welcome. But trulie man, I am angrie with you, and halfe out of patience, that you go not to ſeeke helpe againſt yonder ſame olde beaſt. I haue another hen dead this night. Other men can ſeeke remedy.

B 2                    Here

here is M. B. tels me, that the good wife R. all the laste
weeke could not make her butter come. She neuer rested
vntil she had got her husbande out to the woman at R. H.
and when he came home, they did but heat a spit red hotte,
and thrust into the creame, vsing certaine wordes, as shee
willed him, and it came as kindly as anie butter that euer
she made. I met the olde filth this morning. Lord, how sow-
erlie she looked vpon me, & mumbled as she went, I heard
part of her wordes. Ah (quod she) you haue an honest man
to your husband, I heare how he doth vse me. In trueth,
husband, my stomacke did so rise against her, that I coulde
haue found in my heart to haue flowen vpon her, and scratched her, but that I feared she would be too strong for me.
It is a lustie olde queane. I wished that the good wife R.
had bene with me. I pray you, good husbande, let me intreat you to goe to that same good woman, you may ride
thither in halfe a day.

Sam. Wife, I pray thee be content, I haue intreated
this mine olde friend to reason with M. B. for he tels mee
that we be in a verie foule errour.

M. B. I suppose, so farre as my learning and capacitie doe extend, that small reasoning may serue. The worde
of God doeth shew plainlie that there be witches, & commaundeth they should be put to death. Experience hath
taught too too manie, what harmes they doe. And if anie
haue the gift to minister help against them, shall we refuse
it? Shall we not drinke when we are a thirst? Shall wee
not warme vs when wee are a colde? It is pitie that anie
man should open his mouth anie way to defend them, their
impietie is so great.

Dan. For my part, I go not about to defend witches.
I denie not but that the deuill worketh by them. And that
they ought to be put to death. We ought also to seeke remedie against them: but as I told my friend, the deuil doth
bewitch men by meanes of these witches, and lead them
from

from God, euen to follow himself, to offer sacrifice vnto him to worship him, to obey his wil, to commit manie grieuous sinnes, and to be drowned in manifold errours.

M. B. If you haue this meaning, that witches and sorcerers ar bewitched by the deuil, that they forsake God, and follow him, that they worship and obey him, and doe sacrifice vnto him, and commit manie hainous sinnes, I agrée with you, for I tak it, they euen vow themselues to the deuill, or els he would not be so readie to doe them seruice. But if you mean, that such as seek remedie against them, & wold haue them rooted out, be so seduced and mis-led by the deuill, as you speake, I say your speach is rash and foolish, for they that be earnest against witches, be earnest against the deuil, they defie the deuil, they seek to resist him, and to roote out his instruments. Now, if you were a man that had any learning, you should sée, that contraries cannot be in the same subiect, at one instant, in the same part, and in the same respect: how then can a man hate the deuill, defie the deuill and his workes, and yet follow him at one time?

Dan. I know that witches and coniurers are seduced and become the vassals of Satan: they be his seruants, and not he theirs, as you speake. But I mean indeed that multitudes are seduced and led from God, to follow the deuil, by means of witches & coniurers: yea, I speak it of those, not which are caried of a godlie zeale, but of a blinde rage and mad furie against them. If I speake this rashlie and foolishlie, as you say, and your self learned as you boast, and I vnlearned, I shall be the more easilie ouerthrowne. But I speake so truly, and can so well iustifie all that I haue said by the word of God, that your learning and best skill, shall not be able to disproue the same. Your logicke at the first doth faile you. Not that contraries can be in the same subiect at the same instant, in the same part, and in the same respect. But herein you are vtterly blinde and deceiued, that you name contraries, and take it that the first of

them.

them, as namelie, to hate the deuill, to defie him and his woꝛkes, are in them, when as indeed they are in them but in imagination. Foꝛ if men say and think they defie the deuill and his woꝛkes, and thꝛough blindnes and infidelitie, are euen bewitched, and seduced to followe the deuill, and to do his will, doth their speach and blinde imagination make the things indeed to be in them? What if a pooꝛe begger woman say and thinke that she is a Queene: is she therfoꝛe no begger, begging still her bꝛead? oꝛ is she rid of her lice?

M. B. Nay, if you iudge, I haue done. If men be earneſt againſt the deuill, and defie him and all his woꝛkes, are you to iudge of their conscience, and to say they defie him but in imagination, and follow him, and woꝛship him in deede? is not God alone the iudge ouer mens hearts? Againe, do you compare those that are in their right mind, with such as be mad, oꝛ out of their wits?

Dan. I knowe that God alone is the searcher of the heart, touching the thinges which lie hid in secrete: But where things are open and manifeſt, the tree is known by the fruits, so far as we may goe. As if a man pꝛofesse the faith of Jesus Chꝛiſt soundlie, in all pointes accoꝛding to the woꝛd of God, and doth frame his life thereafter in doing good woꝛkes: it is verie wicked foꝛ anie man to iudge of him, that he is an hypocrite, and that he doth all of vaine gloꝛie. And yet it may be that the Loꝛd, who discerneth the secrete intents of the heart, seeth indeed that he is but an hypocrite. On the contrarie parte, where a man pꝛofesseth in woꝛdes that he doeth defie the deuill and all his woꝛkes, and yet when it commeth to the triall of Gods woꝛd, hee is found to be seduced, and wꝛapped in blinde errours of the deuill, in infidelitie, and euill woꝛks, in which he fulfilleth the will of Satan, and honoureth him in the place of God: Shal we say that this is a good man because of his woꝛds and imagination, that he defieth the deuill and his woꝛks?

Wo

Wo be to them that cal good euil, and euil good. Esa. 5.
We may say they are in bad case, except they repent, and
turne from following Satan. But yet I say, that a faithful
man may erre in some of these thinges through weaknesse
of faith, and through ignorance. And therefore, here men
may not be too rash in iudgment. And now wheras you find
fault, that I make comparison between such as be mad and
those that be in their right mind it is your ignorāce, which
do not consider that ther be two kinds of madnes, or being
out of their right mind, the one for matters of this worlde,
the other for thinges spirituall and heauenlie. There bee
which are in their wittes for this worlde, which touching
spirituall things are as farre awrie in their imaginations,
as the poore beggar, which thinketh she is a goodlie queene.
Doth not the holie Apostle say, that because men receiue
not the loue of the truth, God wil send them strong de-
lusion to beleeue lies. 2. Thess. 2. And what is that, but
that Satan shall seduce, illude and bewitch their minds, to
make them beleeue that they worshippe and follow God,
when they worship and follow him?

M. B. Doe you take that to be S. Paules meaning?
Doth Satan bewitch mens mindes, and leade them into
falsehoode and errour, making them belæue they worshipp
God, when they worship deuils?

Dan. S. Paul speaketh there indéed of the comming
of the great Antichrist in the power of the Deuill. Nowe,
those which are seduced and worship Antichrist, think they
worship God: but marke what S. John sayth, All the
world wondred, and followed the beast, and worshipped the dragon which gaue power to the beast: & they
worshipped the beast. Reuelat. 13. And looke in the 12.
chapter of the Reuelation, and you shall find that the Dragon, which the Poperty doth worship in stead of God, is the
Deuill.

M. B. Trulie I like your wordes well, I am persuaded the deuill doth seduce and bewitch mens mindes: But touching these that seek help at the hands of cunning men and women against witches, I cannot thinke so hardlie of them. I may be awry, I see well: I will not be obstinate, if the word of God shew me mine errour. Let vs euen friendly conferre of the matter. Be not offended with me, and for my part, I will speake all that I knowe or thinke.

Dan. I must intreate you likewise to beare with my plaine speaches. And let vs in the matters proceede from one point to another, standing onlie vpon that, wherein we shall be found to differ in iudgment. And let Gods word be the Iudge betweene vs.

Sam. I like this wel, though I can say but litle, I wil sit and heare you.

Dan. What is the first question that we shal handle?

M. B. I heard you say, if I did not mistake your speach that there be witches that worke by the deuill. But yet I pray you tell me, doe you think there be such? I know some are of opinion there be none.

Dan. It is so euident by the Scriptures, and in all experience, that there be witches which worke by the deuill, or rather I may say, the deuill worketh by them, that such as go about to proue the contrarie, doe shewe themselues but cauillers.

M. B. I am glad we agree in that point, I hope we shall in the rest. What say you to this? that the witches haue their spirits, some hath one, some hath more, as two, three, foure, or fiue, some in one likenesse, and some in another, as like cattes, weasils, toads, or mise, whome they nourish with milke, or with a chicken, or by letting them sucke now and then a drop of blood: whome they call when they be offended with anie, and send them to hurt them in their bodies; yea, to kill them, and to kill their cattell?

Dan. Here is great deceit, and great illusion, here the deuil leadeth the ignorant people into foule errours,

*by*

by which hee draweth them hedlong into manie grieuous sinnes.

M. B. Nay then I ſee you are awrie, if you denie theſe things, and ſay they be but illuſions. They haue bene prooued, and prooued againe, euen by the manifold confeſſions of the witches themſelues. I am out of all doubt in theſe, and could in manie particulars lay open what hath fallen out. I did dwell in a village within theſe fiue yeares, where there was a man of good wealth, and ſuddainlie within ten daies ſpace, he had three kine died, his gelding worth ten pounds fell lame, he was himſelf taken with a gret pain in his back, & a child of ſeuē years old died. He ſent to the woman at R. H. and ſhe ſaid he was plagued by a witch, adding moreouer, that there were three women witches in that towne, and one man witch: willing him to look whom he moſt ſuſpected: he ſuſpected one old woman, and cauſed her to be caried before a Iuſtice of Peace and examined: with much a doe at the laſt ſhee confeſſed all: Which was this in effect: that ſhe had three ſpirits: one like a cat, which ſhe called Lightfoot, another like a Toad, which ſhe called Lunch, the third like a Weaſill, which ſhe called Makeſhift. This Lightfoot, ſhe ſaid, one mother Barlie of W. ſolde her aboue ſixteene yeares agoe, for an ouen cake, and told her the Cat would doe her good ſeruice, if ſhe woulde, ſhe might ſend her of her errand: this Cat was with her but a while, but the Weaſill and the Toad came and offered their ſeruice: The Cat would kill kine, the Weaſill would kill horſes, the Toade would plague men in their bodies. She ſent them all three (as ſhe confeſſed) againſt this man: She was committed to the priſon, and there ſhee died before the Aſſiſes. I could tell you of manie ſuch: I had no minde to dwell in that place any longer.

Dan. You miſtake me, I do not meane that the things are not, but my meaning is, that the deuill by ſuch thinges doth beguyle and ſeduce ignorant men, and lead them into

C                    errours

# A Dialogue concerning

errours and grieuous sinnes: And let vs examine euerie
parcell of that which you set down in your speach, and you
shall sée no lesse.

M. B. That is it which I would faine sée: You confesse
they haue spirits, some one, some moze, and in such like=
nesses: what errour be the people led into by that?

Dan. First, consider this that ther be multituds & armies
of deuils, as we sée in the gospel, y manie deuils wer entred
into one man, & Christ saying, What is thy name? answer
is made, Legion, for we are manie. Mark. 5. Now, al=
though the deuils be manie, yet they be all caried with such
hatred against God, with such desire to haue him dishono=
red and blasphemed, and burne with such bloudy malice
and crueltie against men, that they bend their studie all to=
gether, one helping and furthering another what they can
in their wozke: in so much that the Scripture doeth speake
of them, as if they were but one deuill: foz S. Peter sayth,
Your aduersarie the deuill goeth about like a roring li=
on seeking whom he may deuour. 1. Pet.5. And in the
Reuelation chapter 12. all the deuils make that great red
dzagon: And our Sauiour doth shewe how close they ioyne
in one, when he saith, If Satan be deuided against Satan,
or if Satan cast foorth Satan, how shall his kingdom en=
dure Matth.12. now then, whether the witch deale, as shé
supposeth, with one spirit, oz with manie, it commeth all to
one effect, thus farre, that one dealeth not alone, but with
the helpe of others. So that he oz she that hath familiaritie
with one deuill, it is as much as if it wer with an hundzeth.
Moreouer, the deuils be spirits, they haue no bodily shape
oz likenesse but yet can make an apparance of a shape, as
appeareth by the inchanters befoze Pharao, when their
rods were turned into serpents in shew. Exod.7. And then
one deuill can séem to be foure oz fiue, and foure oz fiue can
séeme to be one: It is therefoze but the craft of Satan, to
make shewe of moze oz lesse.

Doe

*M. B.* Do you not thinke then, that where the moꝛe deuils be, there is the greater power of Satan?

*Dan.* Yes, but it can not be difcerned be his appearing to the witch in ſhew of moꝛe oꝛ leſſe: Foꝛ one can ſéeme ten vnto her, and ten can ſéeme one.

*M. B.* Well, I doe not miſlike al this, I pꝛay you pꝛoceed toꝛwarꝺ.

*Dan.* Then further marke well howe the holie Scriptures doe paint out the deuils to bee mightie terrible ſpirits, full of power, rage, and crueltie, compared to a great fierie red dꝛagon, Reuel. 12. to a greedie oꝛ hungrie lion, that roꝛeth after the pꝛay, 1. Pet. 5. And called by S. Paul Pꝛincipalities, and Powers, the Rulers of the darkneſſe of this woꝛld: now, when they take vpon them the ſhapes of ſuch paltrie vermine, as Cats, Miſe, Toads, and Weaſils, it is euen of ſubtiltie to couer and hide his mightie tyrannie, and power which he exerciſeth ouer the heartes of the wicked. It is moſt neceſſarie foꝛ vs all to know, what ſtrong aduerſaries we haue to encounter withall, that we may fly vnto the Loꝛd God, and ſeek to bee armed with his power againſt them.

*M. B.* Well, what will you inferre vpon this? I cannot deny but that the ſcriptures doe paint out the deuils to be mightie terrible ſpirits, and ſo they may be, although they appeare but like Cats oꝛ weaſils.

*Dan.* I doe not ſay they be not mightie and terrible becauſe they appeare in ſuch ſhapes, but I affirme, that their appearing ſo, is to couer and hide their mightineſſe and effectuall woꝛking, which they exerciſe in the darke harts of men. And marke well I pꝛay you, the power of deuils is in the hearts of men, as to harden the heart, to blinde the eies of the mind, and from the luſtes and concupiſcences which are in them, to inflame them vnto wꝛath, malice, enuy, and cruell murthers: to puffe them vp in pꝛide, arrogancy and vaine gloꝛy: to entice them vnto wantonneſſe,

and whozdomes, and all vncleannesse. And about these
things they wozke continually, and with such efficacy, that
without the power of the glozious passion and resurrecti-
on of our Lozd Jesus Chzist, which we haue by faith, they
cannot be withstood, and they will seeme to be but meane
fellowes, busied about making dzink that it shall not wozk
in the fat, in kéeping chéese from running, and butter from
comming, in killing hennes oz hogges, oz making men
lame.

M. B. Map they not doe both the one and the other?

Dan. Pea, but this is my meaning, that while they be
occupied about the greatest things, as in stirring vp Ty-
rants and wicked men to persecute, to repzoch and blas-
pheme the Gospell, which pulleth them downe, to set diui-
sion and warres between kingdoms and kings, hatred and
discozd between man and wife, and contention betweene
bzethzen:yea, to set all in a bzoyle and confusion:they would
séeme to be busied about trifles, and about these they busie
mens mindes, that they may not obserue and take héed of
them in those other.

M. B. I perceiue your meaning, but yet I doe not
conceiue whereunto you chiefly tend:foz do not they which
looke vpon these harmes done by witches, confesse that the
deuill doth all those things which you mention?

Dan. The ignozant sozt, which are so terrified by witches, do in wozds after a sozt, confesse so much as you say,
but when it commeth to the matter, they deny it in effect.
Foz mark this, the deuils continuallie compasse the soule
of man about, to shoot it full of their fierie dartes. Ephes. 6.
euen to wound it to death with all wicked sinnes. The deuill goeth about like a roring lion, seeking whome hee
may deuour. I. Pet. 5. And they by this craft which they
vse by means of the witches, make the blind people imagin
that they neuer come nigh them, but when the witches are
angrie and doe send them, and that they are easilie dziuen
away

away when they do come, as by burning some quick thing,
as henne, or hogge, or by beating and drawing bloud vpon
the witch. Such people as can thus driue him away, or by
thrusting a spitte red hot into their creame, are farre from
knowing the spirituall battel, in which we are to warre vnder the banner of Christ against the deuill, much lesse doe
they know how to put on (as S. Paule willeth) the whole
armour of God, to resist and ouercome him. Ephes. 6. He
may deale with their soules euen as he listeth, when they
take him not present but vpon such sending, and where
such hurt doth follow in their bodies or goods.

*M. B.* I doe not denie, but that the deuils seeke chiefly
for to destroy the soules of men: But (as I tak it) you confesse, that they being sent by the witches, doe also those bodilie harmes: and as yet I see no reason why they may not
seeke remedie against such harmes, and driue him away by
anie good meanes: doth the worde of God forbid vs to vse
meanes? If I be sicke, shall I not take physicke? If I bee
thirstie, shall I not drinke? Indeed I am of your minde,
though I did neuer marke so much before, that the deuill
dealeth subtillie in this, that by dealing in such small matters, he couereth himselfe in the greater, as though he came
not neere, nor did not medle but in such maner: But here
standeth the case, I resist him in those greater, may I not
also vse those helpes which driue him away in the lesser? I
will if I can driue him away in all things.

*Dan.* Now the deuils are sent by the witches, and how
they doe those bodily harmes, wee are not yet come vnto,
and there lie two of the chiefe subtilties of the deuill in
them, by which he deceiueth the multitude. But by occasion we are fallen into the mention of remedie to driue them
away. Because (I say) such as thus driue him away, know
not the spirituall battell, much lesse how to put on the whol
armour of God to ouercome the deuil: Order doth require
that we speak first of his sending, and then of those bodilie

harmes

harmes which he doth, & afterward of these meanes which are vsed to repell him. Let vs therefore step one step backe againe, if you agrée to the rest which I haue spoken.

M. B. With a good will: for so we shall omit no part. But I thought we had fullie agréd in this, that the witches do send their spirits, and doe manie harmes both vnto men and beasts: because we haue it confirmed by daylie experience: and vnlesse you will denie that which is manifest, I doubt not but we shall accorde in these.

Dan. I say the witches do send their spirits.

M. B. What shal we néd then to stand vpon that point in which we are agréd?

Dan. Yes· though we agree that they send them, yet we may dissent in diuers thinges about this sending. As first, tell me, whether doe you thinke that the witch or the Deuill is the seruaunt, which of them commaundeth, and which obeyeth?

M. B. How can I tell that? It is thought hee becommeth her seruaunt, and where she is displeased, and would be reuenged, she hyreth him for to doe it. The witches théselues haue confessed thus much: and for my part, I thinke no man can disproue it.

Dan. They that doe the will of God are the children and seruants of God. And they which fulfill the lustes of the deuill, and obey him, are his children & his seruantes, Ioh. 8. verf. 44. Act. 13. verf. 10. Are they not?

M. B. I graunt all this?

Dan. The deuilles are the rulers of the darknesse of this world. Ephes. 6. ver. 12.

M. B. The text is plaine.

Dan. The darknesse of this world, is not meant of the darknesse of the night, which is but the shadow of the earth, but it is the spiritual darknes, which consisteth in the ignorance of God, in infidelitie, and in sinne.

M. B. I am of your mind in this also.

Dan.

Dan. And doe you not thinke then that the deuill hath his throne, his dominion and kingdom in the hearts of ignorant blind infidels?

M. B. I must needs thinke he hath, the word of God doth force me thereunto: seeing he is the Prince of darkenesse.

Dan. And is there anie greater infidelitie and darknesse in anie, than in witches, conturers, and such as haue familiaritie with deuils?

M. B. I tak it they be the depest ouerwhelmed in darknesse and infidelitie of all other.

Dan. Lay all these thinges together which you confesse, and see whether it doth not follow vpon the same, that the witch is the vassall of the deuill, and not he her seruant; he is Lord and commaundeth, and she is his drudge and obeyeth.

M. B. Yea, although he be Lord, yet he is content to serue her turne, and the witches confesse, they call them forth and send them: and that they hire them to hurt such in their bodies, and in their cattell, as they bee displeased withall.

Dan. I am sorie you are so farre awrie, it is pitie any man should be in such errour, especiallie a man that hath learning, and should teach others knowledge.

M. B. Nay, I may returne this vpon you, for if you will denie this, it is but a follie to reason any further: I will neuer be driuen from that which I knowe: There was one olde mother W. of great T. which had a spirite like a a Weasill: she was offended highlie with one H. M. home she went, and called forth her spirite, which lay in a pot of woll vnder her bed, she willed him to goe plague the man: he required what she would giue him, and he would kill H. M. She said she would giue him a cocke, which shee did, and he went, and the man fell sicke with a great paine in his bellie, languished and died: the witch was arraigned, condemned, and hanged, and did confesse all this.

*Dan.* I told you before that I do not deny these things, but you are deceiued about the doing: you marke not the cunning sleights of the deuill: Tel me, is not this the truth which S. Peter speaketh, that the deuil goeth about like a roaring lion, seeking whom he may deuoure. 1. Pet. 5.

*M. B.* What then?

*Dan.* What then? can you be so simple as to imagine that the deuill lieth in a pot of wooll, soft and warme, and stirreth not, but when he is hired and sent? The deuils conspire together in their worke, they bestirre them, and neuer take rest night nor day: they are neuer wearie, they be not a colde, they care not for lying soft: These be fooleries by which hee deceiueth the witches, and bewitcheth the mindes of many ignorant people: And whereas you say he is hired, it is but deceit: for, let me aske you two or three questions or more if need be.

*M. B.* What be your questions?

*Dan.* You say the witch commeth home angrie, who hath kindled this wrath in her heart but the deuill? Who inflameth her mind with malice, to be reuenged, and to doe mischiefe but the deuill? doth not he rule in her heart? Tell me what you thinke of this?

*M. B.* I muste needes confesse hee stirreth her vp to wrath and malice.

*Dan.* Then he lieth not at home in his pot of wooll: nor he is not hyred to this: hitherto she is his drudge, and obeyeth him, and not he her, being led by his suggestion. Then tell me, is not the deuill like a red or fierie dragon, Reuel. 12. burning in malice against God, and with all bloodie and cruell hatred that may be against men? And is he not farre readier vnto all mischiefe, than anie man or woman?

*M. B.* The deuill is more fierce than any man or woman; none can deny this.

*Dan.*

*Dan.* If none can deny this, and he be the worker of the wrath and malice in the heart of the witch; then what néedeth he to be hyred: he stirreth her vp, and if he would, he could turn her mind from sending him, and must he be hyred: doth he care for a cock or a chicken: Is he hungry or néedeth he somewhat to eat?

*M. B.* Nay, but it is thought he taketh those thinges to witnesse against the witch that she is his.

*Dan.* Let it bee, there were somewhat in that which you speake, yet he hath a farre déeper reach, for the trueth is, hee woulde, and doeth perswade the blind people, that he medleth litle, but when he is euen hyred and sent, and that then his medling is but in such matters: And here-upon all is on a broyle against old women, which can any wayes be suspected to be witches, as if they were the very plagues of the world, and as if all would be well, and safe from such harmes, if they were rooted out, and thus they fall a rooting out without all care: for it is thought that the witch which hath her spirits, is euen lyke a man which hath curst dogges, which he may set vpon other mens cat-tell, which yet in the nature of dogs, would neuer styrre but when they are bidden: and so the harmes do come from the man which oweth those dogs. They think that the country might be ryd of such spirits, if there were none to hoister them, or to set them a worke. They imagine that they and their cattell should then goe safe. Alas poore creatures, how they be deluded: how litle do they vnderstand the high prouidence of almighty God which is ouer all:

*M. B.* Do you thinke then that witches ought not to be rooted out: or doe you thinke it were not much safety to the country from harmes, if it could be rid of them?

*Dan.* For the rooting out of witches, the Scripture is plaine. Thou shalt not suffer a witch to liue: but we are not yet come to that poynt. But whether they be to be rooted out that men may be safe from harmes, as the peo-

D                                                                                              ple

ple in fury and blindnesse imagine, that is next.

*M.B.* Men feele the smart and the harmes which they
doe, and it is no maruell, though they be earnest to haue
them rooted out, and a good riddance it were if the whole
land could be set free from them.

*Sam.* Trulie M.B. I am of your mind, I wold they wer
all hanged vp one against another: we should not (I hope)
stand in such fear of their spirits. But I interrupt you too.

*The wife.* They that would not haue them hanged or
burnt, I would they might euen witch them vnto hell. If
I had but one fagot in the world, I would carry it a myle
vpon my shoulders to burne a witch.

*Dan.* Well good woman, spare your fagot a while,
and ease your shoulders, and let vs reason the matter a little further. I pray you let me aske you this question, doth
the witch or the deuill the harme vnto men and cattell?

*M.B.* Why, the deuill doth it at their sending though
I confesse it must needs be as you said, that the deuil worketh al in the mind of the witch, & moueth her to send him.

*Dan.* The deuill hath a kingdome, but it is in darkenesse and corruption of sinne. He hath no right nor power
ouer Gods creatures, no not so much as to kill one flye, or
to take one eare of corne out of anie mans barne, vnlesse
power be giuen him. You know when Christ cast the deuils
out of the man possessed, they aske leaue for to goe into the
heard of swine. Then tell me, who giueth the deuill this
power then, when the witch sendeth him, to kill or to lame
man or beast? doth the witch giue it him? Do you think he
had power to doe harme, but no mind till she moued him?
Or doe you take it that her sending giueth him power,
which he had not?

*M.B.* It is a question indeed worth the asking: For
doubtlesse, the deuill hath not power vntill it be giuen him,
to touch any creature, to hurt, or to destroy the body, but
onely to tempt and to lead into sin: I am also sure that the
witch

witch cannot giue him power, but onlie God aboue.

Dan. Lay thefe two together then, that the deuill only hurteth, and that none can giue him power, neither man
no2 woman, but only God, and tell me whether the people
be not wonderfully carried away in a rage. Fo2, when as
they fhould confider, that the deuill is the Lo2des execution-
ner: And then finding that he hath any power giuen him
to moleft, to hurt and vexe them in they2 bodies o2 goods,
to know certainly it commeth from the Lo2d, and then ga-
ther from thence (as the trueth is) that the Lo2d is displea-
fed with them fo2 their offences. And fo feeke vnto him,
humbly crauing pardon and deliuerance from this enemy,
feeking to be armed with the mighty power of faith, to caft
him foo2th, and to refift him, as the Lo2d willeth, 1. Pet. 5
Here is no fuch matter, no looking fo high among the people, but running deeper into errour, and into finne, as if the
witches did it, and that it commeth from their anger and
not from their owne finnes and infidelity, here is no repentance, no humbling themfelues by fafting and p2ayer,
but running fo2 helpe vnto deuilles, vfing meanes which
thofe deuils by the cunning men & women appoint, fcrat-
ching and clawing, thirfting often after guiltles blood as
raging againft thofe whome they imagine to be witches,
which many times are not, becaufe they imagine, that if
there were no witches, ther fhould be no fuch plagues. As
if they had no foule finnes no2 vnbeleefe, o2 that there re-
mayned not a iuft reuenging God to punifh, o2 as if he had
not the deuils ftill the executioners of his w2ath.

M. B. Truly your wo2des doe make me affrayd: fo2
I am euen guiltie of thofe thinges my felfe, if they be fo
grieuous, as you fet them out: and by Gods grace I wil
confider better of the matter: fo2 I haue counfelled manie
to feek vnto thofe cunning folkes, and to vfe fuch helpes as
they p2efcribe, and you fay, it is to feeke help at deuils. To
fee that point we fhal come anon: now I wold be refolued

about somewhat in your last speach ; as namely, doe you cleare the witches, because God, and not they, giueth the deuil power, and doe you thinke that the deuils should kill men and their cattell, if they were not sent by witches? Should the harmes still follow, if there were no witches?

Dan. That I say God alone, and not the witches, giueth power vnto the deuils to plague and torment: it is so euident as that I suppose a man shall hardlie meete with anie man so grosse but will confesse it. But this doeth not cleare the witches at all ; for their sinne is in dealing with deuils, and that they imagine that their Spirits do those harmes, requested and hyred by them: when as indeede the deuill, where he hath power giuen him to hurt, or where he knoweth death or grieuous diseases will follow either in man or beast, setteth the witch in a rage, and moueth her to send him. Concerning your other question, I say, we shall finde by the Scriptures, that if there were no witches at all, yet men should be plagued by the deuils in their bodies and goods. For touching the godly, the Lord doth vse Satan to afflict them in their bodies and in their goodes, for to trie their faith and patience : as the example of holie Iob doeth testifie in ample maner. It were vile follie and brutish to affirme, that witches did set on the deuils to kill his children, and to plague his bodie. And I hold it no smal follie, for anie man to think that the Lord doeth not nowe scourge his children, at the least some of them, for their good, by the deuill. There is no doubt, but the deuill hauing power giuen him to afflict, vseth all the craft hee can, and will seek to be sent by the witch, and so hee will make it knowne, because it may seeme to bee not from God, but from the anger of a poore woman. And now touching the wicked, which prouoke God by their wicked sinnes and vnbeleefe, may we not read in the scriptures that an euill spirite was sent of God vnto king Saul, which did haunt and vexe him? Was this spirit sent by a witch? Or the deuils

tils in the Gospell, which entred into the hearde of swine
and drowned them? Did the Lord giue them power, and
send them, and shall we be so sottish as to thinke, that hee
sendeth not the deuill now against vngodly men, to plague
and to destroy them? As I said before, here is the deepe
craft of Satan, that he will couet to bee sent by witches,
whereas indeed God hath sent him, seeing none can sende
him but God. Againe, wee must consider that there bee
naturall causes in the bodies of men and beastes of grieuous tormentes and diseases, yea euen causes of death.
Nowe, they cannot be so secrete, but the deuill knoweth
them, and euen when they are like to take effect. Then doth
he plie it with the witch, setteth her in a furie, she sendeth
him, euen vpon this sending the man or the beast suddainlie and strangely are tormented, fall lame, or die. Then the
witch is suspected, examined, and confesseth that she killed
such a man, or such a mans cattell, or made them lame.
Here the people are set in a wonderfull maze and astonish-
ment, as if witches could plague men in their wrath, by
sending their spirits, because they confesse they did it, whē
their spirits doe lie and had no power, but the tormentes
came by naturall causes. And to driue the people into a
deeper madnes in this, & to mak them beléue, that strange
and suddaine torments and languishing diseases come by
witches, he hath his other sort of witches, the cunning men
and women, which tell euen vpon his worde, which you
know is to be trusted, that they be bewitched, that they bee
haunted with fayries, and that ther be thus many witches
therabout, in euerie town some.

    M. B. That is most true no doubt, which you speake,
I doe not for my part knowe how to gainsay any one point
thereof. Only I wonder at the craftinesse of the deuils in
these things, that where they haue power graunted vnto
them to hurt, they wil be sent by the witches, as if they did
it hired by them, and that you say where harmes doe fol-
                         low

low men vpon naturall causes, that they can make shew as though they did them. But are you of this mind, that there should be as manie or all those harmes done by deuilles, if there were no witches, as there be now? Although I must needs confesse, that the witches can giue the deuil no power, nor he can take none by their sending: yet may it not bee that God giueth them power oftener because of those witches dealing with them, than if there were no witches at all?

Dan. The craftinesse of deuils is such, as without the light of Gods worde, the wisest men vnder heauen muste needes be deceiued thereby. We sée there be some men so déep in subtilties and can carie matters so close, that men can not discerne them: how much more the deuilles, which are excéedingly subtill, & craftie aboue the subtillest men? the question which you aske is (in my iudgment) somwhat hard: But this is vndoubted, that if the Lord God do giue vnto the deuils oftener power to hurt because of the witches, I meane because the deuils doe deale by such instruments, it is in his heauie iudgment against the wickednes of the people, which despise the true and heauenlie light of his word. As S. Paule (prophecying of the comming of the great Antichrist) sheweth, that because men did not receiue the loue of the trueth, God gaue the deuill power by Antichrist and his ministers, to seduce by lying signes and wonders. Indéed, I will not say that for the witch the deuill hath power giuen him, but for the wickednesse of the people, which deserue that by witches the deuill shoulde haue power to seduce them further. Here yet we muste take héede of the common errour which a multitude are caried so hedlong withall, that they can by no means sée, that God is prouoked by their sinnes to giue the deuill such instruments to work withall, but rage against the witch, euen as if she could do all.

M. B. Surelie, I should bee a wretch to deny, that
God

God giueth the Deuilles power to plague and to seduce because of mens wickednes ; but yet I would knowe whether a godly faythfull man or woman may not bee bewitched? Wee see the deuill had power giuen him ouer Iob?

Dan. This example of Iob is not fit to prooue that a godly man may be bewitched, seeing the deuill is not sayde to deale by witches against him, but it doeth prooue, that not only the godlie, but euen the most godly (as holy Iob, who had none like him vpon earth) may for their triall be giuen into the handes of Satan to be afflicted and tempted. And as I said, where Satan hath power granted him of God, to strike with bodily plagues any of the godly, for the triall of their fayth and patience, he will couet, if he can bring it about, to bee sent by some witch, and to haue it knowne that he was sent. But the faithfull are to turne their eies from the witch, and to deale with God, for from him the matter commeth. When they be tried, the Lord in his good time will deliuer them depending vpon him, to their great praise and glory, euen as valiant souldiers. It is therefore, of no great force, whether Satan come from the witch against the godlie, or whether he haue no witch to deale by: ouercome thou the deuill, and thou ouercommest all. Indeed among the more ignorant sort he preuayleth much, when he toucheth those which imbrace the liuely word as sent from a witch. For many nowe doe euen quake and tremble, and their faith doth stagger. Hath hee power (thinke they) ouer such as be cunning in the scriptures, then what are they the better for their profession? the witch is on their bones as well as vpon others. By this it might seeme, and so they take it, that other helpes and remedies are to be sought than by the scriptures. And so they run and seeke help where they ought not.

M. B. Then I pray you, though I be already perswaded it is naught to seeke to these cunning men for help against witches, yet let vs conferre a little of that. There

be

be diuers things which haue perſuaded me to thinke marueilous well of them, and euen as of ſuch as God hath giuen wiſedome and ſkill vnto, euen for to doe much good.
For we ſee many receiue help by them, and are deliuered
from the plagues which come by deuils. And firſt, I wold
know how they can bee ſo earneſt againſt witches, if they
deale with the deuill, and ſo be indeed witches themſelues?
how can they haue any mind in charity to doe good, to take
pitie vpon ſuch as be in miſery? Or how will Satan driue
forth Satan? For they no doubt, driue out deuilles out of
ſome.

Dan. I would come to aunſwere your queſtions touching the ſeeking help at the hands of cunning men or women, but tell me firſte, are you reſolued touching the ſending of the ſpirits, and touching the harms that are done?
Me think you ſlip too ſuddainly from theſe points?

M. B. I cannot tell whether I vnderſtand your meaning in euery thing, but ſure, I haue bene in error greatly I muſt needs confeſſe. And if you pleaſe, we may ſtande
ſomewhat longer in theſe queſtions.

Sam. Indeed it is my deſire that you woulde ſpeake a
litle playner of theſe poyntes: for I haue marked well all
your talke, and cannot well conceiue of the laſt things you
dealt in. With your leaue M. B. I would aſke two or
three queſtions of my friend. Here was but ſeuen miles
hence at W. H. one M. the man was of good wealth, and
well accounted of among his neighbours. He pined away
with ſickneſ halfe a yeare, and at laſt died. After hee was
dead, his wife ſuſpected ill dealing: ſhe went to a cunning
man, I know not where, and deſired to know whereof her
huſband died. He told her that her huſband died of witcherie: he aſked her if ſhe did not ſuſpect any therabout. She
ſayd there was one woman which ſhe did not like, one mother W. her huſband and ſhe fell out, and he fell ſick within two dayes after, and neuer recouered again. He ſhewed
her

her the woman as plaine in a glasse, as we see one another,
and in the very apparell she went in at that hower, for shee
ware an old red cappe with corners, such as women were
wont to weare; and in that she appeared in the glasse: Hee
taught her how she might bring her to confesse. Well, she
followed his counsell, went home, caused her to be apprehended and caried before a Justice of peace. He examined
her so wisely, that in the end she confessed shee killed the
man. She was sent to prison, she was arraigned, condemned, and executed: And vpon the ladder shee seemed very
penetent, desiring all the world to forgiue her. She said
she had a spirit in the likenes of a yellow dun catte. This
catte came vnto her, as she said, as she sat by her fire, when
she was fallen out with a neighbour of hers, and wished
that the vengeance of God might light vpon him and his.
The catte bad her not be affraid, she wold do her no harme:
She had serued a dame fiue peares in Kent, that was now
dead, and if she would, she would be her seruant. And wheras, said the Cat, such a man hath misused thee, if thou wilt
I will plague him in his cattell. She sent the Cat, she killed three hogs and one Cow. The man suspecting, burnt a
pig aliue, and as she said, her cat wold neuer go thither any
more. Afterward she fel out with that M. she sent her Cat,
who told her, that she had giuen him that, which hee should
neuer recouer: and indeed the man died. Now doe you not
thinke the woman spake the trueth in all this? Would the
woman accuse her selfe falsely at her death? Did not the
Cat become her seruant? Did not she send her? Did shee
not plague and kill both man and beaste? What shoulde a
man thinke of this?

Dan. You propounde a particular example, and let
vs examine euery thing in it touching the witch, for the
womans fact that went to the wise man, wee are not yet
come to that point. You say the Cat came to her when she
was in a great rage with one of her neighbours, and did
E curse,

curſe, wiſhing the vengeance of God to fall vpon him and
his.

Sam. She ſaid ſo indéede. I heard her with mine own
ears, for I was at the execution.

Dan. Then tel me who ſet her in ſuch a deuiliſh rage,
ſo to curſe & banne, as to wiſh that the vengeance of God
might light vpon him and his? did not the Cat?

Sam. Trulie I thinke the Deuil wrought that in her.

Dan. Uerie well, then you ſée the Cat is the beginner
of this play.

Sam. Cald you it a play? It was no play to ſome.

Dan. Indeed the witch at laſt had better haue wrought
hard, than bene at her play. But I meane Satan did play
the Jugler: For, doth he not offer his ſeruice? Doth he not
moue her to ſend him to plague the man? Tell me, is ſhe ſo
forward to ſend, as he is to be ſent? Or doe you not take it,
that he ruleth in her heart, and euen wholly directeth it to
this matter?

Sam. I am fully perſwaded he ruleth her heart.

Dan. Then was ſhee his drudge, and not he her ſer-
uant, he needeth not to be hired nor intreated, for if her hart
were to ſend him any where, vnto ſuch as he knoweth hee
cannot hurt, nor ſeeth how to make any ſhewe that he hurteth them, he can quickly turne her from that. Wel, the cat
goeth and killeth the man, certain hogs and a Cow: howe
could ſhe tell that the Cat did it?

Sam. How could ſhe tell? why he told her man, and the
law and heard that he loſt his cattell.

Dan. The Cat would lie, would ſhe not? for they ſay
ſuch cattes are lyers.

Sam. I doe not truſt the Cats wordes, but becauſe the
thing fell out ſo.

Dan. Becauſe the hogges and the Cow died, are you
ſure the Cat did kil them, might they not die of ſome naturall cauſes as you ſée both men and beaſts are well, and die
ſud-

suddainlie?

*Sam.* That were strange, if they should die of naturall causes, and fall out so fit at the time after he was sent?

*Dan.* It is not straunge at all, as marke what I tell you and you shall easily sée. There bee naturall causes of tortures and griefe, of lamenes, and of death in the bodies of men and beastes, which lie so hid and secrete, that the learneddest Physitians can not espie them, but the deuill séeth them, and can coniecture very neere the time, when they will take effect. Then doeth hee ply it, to bring the matter about that it may séeme he did it. If hee haue any witch to deale by, he stirreth vp some occasion to set her in a rage with that partie: and then he will be sent, and telleth her he doeth it. If he haue no witch to deale by, yet hee will set debate betwéene the partie and some other, whom he may bring into suspition, as his greatest desire is to haue innocent bloud shed.

*Sam.* Here is a matter brought about indéed, how could the Cat doe all this?

*Dan.* I told you before, that the deuilles worke together, and can spéedilie and most craftilie compasse thinges, which are farre beyond the reach of mans capacitie. But sometime the deuill hath power giuen him to plague and doth the harme. Admit he had power giuen him, and did kill the cattell of this man: let vs come nowe to that, who think you, gaue him the power for to strike and kill? Did the witch giue him the power, or the Lord God?

*Sam.* Nay surely, the witch cannot giue him power.

*Dan.* Did he receiue power after she sent him?

*Sam.* That cannot I tell.

*Dan.* Thē mark a litle: he hath power giuē him to plague this man in his goods: he wil do it, but he will doe it craftily. The Lord gaue him power ouer the goods of holie Iob: he worketh by instruments, for he stirreth vp the Sabeis, and they take away his Oxen, and his Asses: he raiseth vp

E 2                                           also

also the Chaldeis, and they cary away his Camels, Iob. 1.
Euen so, hauing power to strike, he wil be sent by a witch,
he could doo it without her, but he gayneth much that way,
as we shall seé when wee come to speake of the remedyes
which men seeke.

Sam. I wonder then that the man neuer had more hurt
after he had burnt his pig aliue:

Dan. O man, the Deuill can abide no roast meate, nor
no fire, he is affraide, if they fall a roasting, that they will
roast him. If they run at him with a spit red hot, they gas-
ter him so sore, that his dame shal go her self, if she will, he
will come no more there. But of these thinges we are to
speake afterward in their place.

Sam. You make the deuill wonderfull subtill.

Dan. He is so subtill and full of all craft and sleight,
that no earthly creature can escape from being seduced by
him, without the light of Gods heauenly word. But let vs
come now to the other man, whom the witch confessed shee
killed by her Cat.

Sam. Yea, that me thinketh is more than the other,
the woman was told by the cunning man that her husband
was killed by witcherie. The witch confessed so much at
her death. The Cat told the witch, that she killed him.

Dan. Here be a companie of credible persons to be beleeued: the cunning man saith the man was bewitched to
death. Who told him that:

Sam. His spirite that maketh the witch appeare in the
glasse.

Dan. That same Spirite, what doe you take him to
be, an Angell, or a Deuill:

Sam. Some of the cunning men say, they haue Moses
or Elias, or the Spirite of some holy man.

Dan. The Deuill can turne himselfe into the liknes
of an Angell of light. For they that doe thinke the cunning
men and women deale with any other Spirite than Sa-

                                                        tan

tan, haue no vnderstanding. Satan saith, the man was witched to death.

Sam. Satan saith so, he is not to bee beleeued, but the witchconfesseth it was so.

Dan. Who told the witch?

Sam. Her Cat that she sent.

Dan. What is the Cat, a deuill? then remember the prouerbe, aske his fellow if he be a theefe. All the matter resteth vpon the testimony of deuils, and they not put to their oath. Wee will not ground vpon mans testimonie without an oath, and must we beleeue the bare worde of deuils?

Sam. Do you thinke then that the man was not killed by witcherie?

Dan. It may be the Lord had giuen Satan power to plague the man in his bodie, and then he vnder a colour would be sent by a witch. But it is most like that his bodie did languish and pine of naturall causes, which the deuill did know, and so would be sent, and seeme to do all, when as indeed he had no power to touch him. For, although the Lord giue the deuill power, to strike some in their bodies for their haynous sinnes, yet the most which the witches thinke their spirits doe kill at their request, doe die of naturall diseases.

Sam. Then it seemeth the witches are deceiued, and mocked, when he maketh them beleeue he doeth kill and plague when hee doeth not. And againe in this, where he hath power giuen him of God, to strike man or beast, hee could doe it, and would without the witch, and so vseth the witch for a collour to draw on worse matters.

Dan. I am glad you take my meaning so right: for, thinke deeply of the matters, and you shall see it must needs be so.

Sam. I interrupted M. B. I pray you goe forward now to the rest.

E 3                                        Dan.

# A Dialogue concerning

**Dan.** Our matter which we come vnto nowe, is the helpe and remedie that is sought for against witches at the hands of cunning men. And now if it please you to propound your questions, I will answere to them the best I can.

**M. B.** Nay truly, I see already all is naught, but yet I will obiect those things which haue caried me awrie. I take it a man is to seek remedy against euils, & I thought it was euen a gift that God gaue vnto those whom we cal cunning men, that they did very much good by. When a thing is lost, when a thing is stollen, many goe to them, and they help them to it. I did know where the Communion cup was stollen: the Churchwardens rode to a wise man, he gaue them direction what night, and where they should stand, and the party that had stollen it should come thither, and confesse he had it: and certainly they had it againe. I did know one that had a child of fiue yeares old, a gyrle, it was taken piteouslie: the father was in great heauinesse, and knew not what to doe: some gaue him counsell to goe to a woman which dwelt ten miles from him, and to carie some of the clothes which the child lay in: he did so, the woman told him that his child was bewitched, and if hee did not seeke remedie in time, the childe would be lost: Shee bad him take some olde clothes, and let the child lie in them all night, and then take and burne them: and he should see by the burning, for if they did burne black, that shewed the child was bewitched, and she said further, that doubtlesse the witch would come thither: he followed her aduice, and sure as we be here, there came an old woman in, which he suspected, euen while they were burning, and made an errand: the man made no more adoe, but euen laid his clowthes vpon her and clawed her vntill the blood ranne down her cheeks, and the child was well within two dayes after. I could tell you of a stranger thing, but I haue it but by report, but yet indeed by very credible report. There was

a

# witches and witchcraftes.

a butcher by his trade that had a boy to his sonne, his name was John, grieuous sores did breake forth vpon him: they laid salues, and none woulde cleaue for to draw or to ease them. The father making his moane to a friend of his, he told him whether he should goe to a verie skilfull man: he did goe, and being demanded whom he suspected, she was shewed him in a glasse, an old woman that dwelt not farre from him in an house alone: he told the cunning man, that the woman had shut vp her dore, & was gone from home out of the shyre, and so he could not tell how to come by her. he told him a way how he, should fetch her home. Cut off the hair (said he) of the boyes head, and put it in a cloath and burne it, and I warrant you she wil come home with al the spæd she can. Burne it abroade, burne it not in a chimney, for if you doe, it will make you all affraide. The man went home and did this. The woman came home with all spæde, came to his house, came to the boy, and saide, John, scratch me, hee scratched her vntil the blood followed, and whereas before nothing would draw his soares, they healed of themselues. What should a man thinke of such things?

*Dan.* You tell of some, which haue receiued help from the hands of cunning men: And no doubt there may infinit examples be brought. Some haue lost, some haue thinges stollen from them, some are vexed in their bodies: They come by the things againe which were lost or stollen, they are taught to doe certain things, and are eased from their griefs. But this we must first knowe, they receiue their helpe, if it deserue the name to be called help, from the deuill. And do you thinke a man may lawfullie seek helpe at the hands of the deuill?

*M. B.* Some are perswaded that they doe not sæke helpe at the hand of deuils, when they goe to the wise men: but that it is a gift which God hath giuen them, euen to do good withall.

E 4                    Dan.

*Dan.* I doe verilie thinke that manie of the people are so perſwaded: but what reaſon is there foz it? Doeth God by his Spirit tell where the thing is which is loſt, oz ſtollen? Is it an Angell from heauen, oz the ſoule of ſome man that is dead, which appeareth in the Chzyſtall, oz in the glaſſe, and ſheweth the image of the partie which hath ſtollen, oz that is a witch?

*M. B.* I had rather heare what you thinke touching theſe things, than ſhew what I haue thought.

*Dan.* The deuils did make the heathen people beleeue that they were goddes, and ſo pzocured that they ſhoulde wozſhip them with diuine wozſhip. Thzough their craftines they had many wayes to eſtabliſh this: they conueied themſelues into images, and out of them gaue anſweres, when they wer demanded, herein they vſed great craft, foz whereas they could not tell what ſhould fall out, they framed the ozacle in ſuch ſozt as it was doubtfull, and might be taken both waies: and ſo looke which part it fell out on, that ſeemed and was taken to be the meaning of the gods. If they did know how things would fal out indeed, as they did know ſundzy things touching the kingdomes and monarchies of the wozld, by the wzitings of the Pzophetes, and diuers things by coniectures, as the deuill could tell Saul he ſhould be ſlaine, becauſe he ſaw God had caſt him off, and the hearts of the Iſraelits fainted, and the Philiſtims were full of courage, thoſe they would tell plainelie. Alſo they did conuey themſelues into the bodies of men and women, and vtter thinges which ſeemed very diuine, ſuch (as I am perſwaded) were the Pzophetiſſes the Sibylles among the heathen. Such was the maide at Philippos, which is mentioned in the Actes of the Apoſtles, which bzought great gain vnto her maiſters by deuining, out of whom Paule caſt the deuill. This maide could tell of things loſt, of things ſtollen, and ſuch like, and great reſozt there was vnto her, as men had neede, oz deſired to

ſee

see the strangenesse of the matter.

*M. B.* Let me interrupt you a litle? The deuill can not be in all places at once : how could he then, remaining in the maide, tell what was done in places farre off? howe can the deuill tel where the thing lost or stollen is, which is not only farre off, but hidden? how can he shewe the image of the thiefe or witch? Can he sit and behold all thinges a farre off, and in secrete?

*Dan.* We may not ascribe vnto Deuils that they can be in all places at once, or sit in one place and beholde all things done a farre off. But they ioyne together in this speciall worke, to set vp their kingdome, and to drawe the people after them, to seeke helpe at their handes, and so to worship them. Some of them be in one place, and some in another, and from all places doe stir vp the faithlesse people to run for helpe to those cunning men, and then they make the relation, for they goe thither also, they know the thiefe whome they mooued to the theft, and can make resemblance of his face and apparell: they can tell where things be that are hid, hauing had a finger in the matter. And thus one spirite, as it doeth seeme, telleth things spoken and done farre off, but it is otherwise, there be manie that doe it, which resort from all the places where the things are done.

M. B. I am satisfied touching this point. You were shewing howe the deuils did deale among the heathen out of the Idols, and out of men and women.

*Dan.* Yea, and they haue subtillie wound themselues in againe among Christians. For vsing witches as their instruments, they make them beleue that they doe manie harmes sent by them, which they do not, and whereas they haue power giuen them by God to afflict, they will seeme to doe it at the wrath and displeasure of the witch, she must send him, the matter must one way or other appeare, eyther he will seeme euen compelled by force of such as do ad-

F        ture

iure him, to confesse that such a woman oz such a man sent him, oz els the witch must confesse so much. Then the people deuise how they may be safe against the witch, there is running to the wisardes to learne what they should doe to withstand the furie of the witch, that she send not to them, oz if she haue sent, how they may expell her spirit, and keep her from sending him againe: this is it which the deuill would haue: foz now he vttereth all his wares: he teacheth by these cunning men and women, many hozrible abhominations, and foule abuses of the name of God, by which they are made beleeue, that they haue remedie against the deuils sent by the witches, and that they are cured from their harmes.

*M. B.* I doe not see how any man can indeed iustifie, oz maintaine, that the spirits which appeare vnto them in the Chzistall, oz in the glasse, oz water, oz that any way do speake, and shewe matters vnto them, be holy Angels, oz the soules of excellent men, as of Moses, Samuel, Dauid, and others, though I haue heard that the cunning men, take them to be such, and thinke they deale by them against deuils.

*Dan.* It is no matter what Satans vassals are made to beleeue by his subtil sleights: it is most abhominable foz any Chzistian man, euer to let it enter into his thought, that they doe any thing by the power oz wisdome of the holie Ghost, by any Angel oz good spirit, oz that they doe any thing against the deuill, which wozke by the intelligence which they haue from euill spirits: therfoz hold this, that they seeke vnto deuils, which run vnto those southsayers.

*M. B.* I am perswaded indeed that they seek vnto deuils, but I would see some reason foz it out of Gods wozd.

*Dan.* Touching all spirituall matters, as to be armed with power against deuils, and to know how to auoid the daungers which they bzing, we are no where to seeke, and to learne but of our most blessed Lozde God. And of
him

him we cannot learn, but by his holy word, for in it he hath opened vnto vs all his whole will. And therefore, where the Lorde commaundeth the people of Israell by Moses, Deut. 18. that they should not when they came into the land, learn to do according to the abhominations of those heathen, reckoning vp sundry kinds of such as were Satans instruments which he vsed to seduce the multitude, by deuinations, by obseruing of times, by augurie, by iuglings with the helpe of the deuill, by vsing familiar Spirits, spirits of deuination, and séeking to the dead : he setteth downe also the remedie, shewing first, that he woulde cast out those nations because they harkened vnto the southsayers, and deuiners, pronouncing that euerie one which doth those things, is an abhomination to the Lorde, willing his people that they should not harken to such, but that they should hearken vnto him : And then Moses saith, A Prophet shall the Lord thy God raise vp vnto thee from among you of thy brethren like vnto me, him shal ye heare.

*M. B.* Then you proue by that place, that we muste séeke only to God, and not to such as work by meanes besides his words.

*Dan.* If you read that place, Deut. 18. and mark euery thinge well, you shall sée it doeth not onely proue that they séeke vnto Deuilles, which runne to these cunning men and women : because the Prophetes which God hath raysed vp to declare the Lords will, commaund vs not to doe such things: but also declareth that they bee an abhomination to the Lorde that vse them, or that séeke vnto them.

*M. B.* I sée then it is not onelie a sinne, but a moste horrible sinne, to séeke vnto them. Alas, many do not think that they séeke vnto deuilles, when they goe for helpe vnto them for thinges stollen, or for helpe and remedie against witches.

# A Dialogue concerning

Dan. No doubt many refuse to hear the voyce of God, to be instructed by him: they despise his word, and therfore they be giuen vp to hearken vnto Deuilles. Such as haue sought vnto any of these that worke by the deuill, and now come to see their offence, ought to shew repentance for the same, not as for a light sinne. It is no small abhomination to goe for helpe vnto the deuill: It is to set him in Gods place, and to honour him as God. It riseth of infidelity and distrust of help from God, as we may see in the example of king Saule, who finding no answere nor comforte from God, whome he had so wickedly disobeyed, went to a witch. The heathen man saide, *Flectere si nequeo Superos, Acheronta mouebo.* If I cannot intreat the goddes, I will downe among the deuils.

M.B. Nay, doubtles there can be no defence made for such seeking help at their hands, which deale with familiar spirits, but I muse at diuers thinges, as this for one, how the cunning men, if they deale by the power of the deuill, should vse such good wordes, and will them that come vnto them to doe all in the name of Christ, teaching them to vse words and sentences of the scriptures.

Dan. O sir, here lieth the deep subtiltie of Satan, how should the people be seduced to follow him, if he should not vse great cunning to couer matters, as if deuils were driuen out, and harmes cured that are done by them, euen through the name and mightie power of God. Herein also lyeth a more foule abhomination, and that is the abusing and horrible prophaning of the most blessed name of God, and the holie Scriptures vnto witcheries, charmes, and coniurations, and vnto all deuillish artes. Such an one is haunted with a fayrie, or a spirit: he must learne a charme compounded of some straunge speaches, and the names of God intermingled, or weare some part of S. Johns Gospell or such like. So against the thiefe, against the deuill sent by the witch, thelike is practized. What can Satan de=

defire moze, than that holie thinges fhould be thus abufed?
There is adoe to get him into the glaffe, to get him into
the Chryftall, to get him into the bafen of water: there is a
doe to binde him, as it were by the name & power of Chrift
to tell this thing oz that thing. The coniurer hee bindeth
him with the names of God, and by the vertue of Chriftes
paffion and refurrection, & fo maketh him ferue his turne:
And all is his owne wozke, foz he is not conftrayned, noz
bound, but feeketh thus to haue God blafphemed. O (fayth
the fimple man) this is a good woman, fhee fpeaketh of
God, and of Chrift, and doth all in his name: they be good
wozds which fhe hath taught me to vfe: and what hurt can
there be in vfing good wozdes? Alas pooze man, what cafe
are they in which muft learne good wozds of the deuill? It
is not the fpeaking of good wozdes, oz the wearing fome
part of the fcriptures, that defendeth from deuils, therein
lieth the craft of fatan, to haue thofe holy thinges fo foullie
abufed, and that men may put truft in wozdes and fenten-
ces pzonounced, but the deuilles are withftood onlie by the
power of faith, where the holie fcriptures are wzitten in
the heart, & the foule armed with the power of them. From
this Satan dzaweth men by his foothfayers, teaching
them other helpes: Foz the naming of God, oz the fenten-
ces of fcripture bindeth not fatan, when wee reade he can
vtter them.

M. B. Then howe can the deuill beare fuch a pitifull
minde, as to help thofe that bee in miferp? Foz many haue
helpe by thefe cunning men. The deuill is cruell and bent
wholly to doe hurt, and that is it which perfwadeth manie
that things are done euen by the power of God.

Dan. The deuils be as pitifull as a greedy hungrie lion that roareth after his pzay, and as a fierce Dzagon, all
burning with wzath and bloody malice: they make fhew of
doing good vnto men, only of a moft cruel and murtherous
purpofe, euen to dzaw men deeper into the pit of hell with

them,

them. For if they can help the bodie a litle, it is to win both bodie and soule vnto eternall damnation. Where satan offereth his help, it is more to be feared, than where he manifestly impugneth, and seeketh apparantly to hurt.

*M.*B. But this then is more strange, if they doe not deale by the power of God, but by the power of the deuill, when they driue out deuils from hurting, howe one deuill should driue out another. Our sauiour saith, that satan doth not driue out satan, for then his kingdom should bee deuided and could not stand.

Dan. It is most certaine that satan doth not driue out satan: for our sauiour hath shewed the reason of the contrarie. One deuill is readie to further the worke of another: but in no wise to expel or to hinder one another.

*M.*B. There is it which maketh me to muse: we see the deuill driuen out, and doeth not returne againe, and if it be not wrought by the power of deuilles, as you say it cannot, then must it needs be by the power of God.

Dan. The Deuill is driuen out, neither by the power of the deuill, nor yet by the power of God, in these that are healed by cunning men.

*M.*B. I like this worst of al the speach which I heard you vtter yet: For if satan be not driuen out neither by the power of satan, nor by the power of God, what other power is there to driue him out? If you can shewe a third power to expell him, it is more than euer I heard of.

Dan. There needeth not a thirde power to expell him, for he is not driuen out at all.

M.B. I told you before, if you denie that to be, which all experience doth shewe, then is it no reasoning. There be examples in many places, and daylie it is seene, that the deuill is driuen out of some possessed, that where he did vexe and torment men in their bodies, and in their cattle, they haue remedie against him.

Dan. I doe not denie but that some which are possessed

sed and tormented by Satan, haue releafe: but yet the deuill is not caft foorth by those means, but ceaseth willingly
euen to establish men in errour, and in moft wicked prophaning of the name of God, and worshipping of himselfe,
and so entreth deeper into them.

M. B. I befeech you let me heare how that is, that you
fay he ceafeth of his owne accord. Will he let goe his hold
willingly and of his owne accord, where he hath it vpon a-
ny man? Doth he not defire to doe hurt?

Dan. He doeth not let goe his hold which he hath vpon
any man, but indeed taketh fafter holde when hee feemeth to
ve caft foorth and doth greater hurt: for tell me whose deuife
is the coniuration?

M. B. I am out of doubt that coniuration is the de-
uice of the deuill.

Dan. Then tell me, hath the deuill deuifed and taught
a way to bind himselfe, or to caft foorth himselfe?

M. B. That I suppose he would neuer doe.

Dan. Indeed if we wil imagine that the deuil is becom
an old foole, we may think he wold teach that which should
bind and caft foorth himselfe: but the fcripture calleth him
the old serpent: he deuifed and taught coniuration, therefore coniuration doth not caft him foorth. Yet he feemeth to
be bound by the coniurer, yea euen by the name of God, and
by the power of the paffion of Chrift. The coniurer feemeth
by the same power to driue him out of a man poffeffed,
whose body he doth vex & torment. And he ceaseth willingly
to torment the bodie, to establish coniuration, & so to draw
men quite from God, euen to worship and to follow himselfe, and feeke all helpes at his hands. Euen so when men
are tormented in their bodies, or plagued in their cattell
by the deuill, and feeke vnto the cunning men and women,
following the way that they prefcribe vnto them, and haue
eafe in their bodies, and no more harme among their cattell, Satan doth not giue place as forced, but ceaseth to do

those

thofe bodilie harmes, that he may fullie win vnto himfelfe
both bodie and foule. If they fhould not feeme to bee expelled, how fhould men be drawn to feek help at their handes
which deale by him: how fhould witches and coniurers be
drawne on moft horriblie to pollute and blafpheme the glorious name of God?

M. B. Then I fee they buy their help deer which haue
it at the handes of thefe cunning men.

Dan. Yea, what can be bought more deare, than that
which is with the loffe of foule and bodie for euer, by running from God after deuils?

M. B. What fhoulde a man thinke then touching all
other which deale not with the deuill, and yet haue certaine
waies to finde out witches, and to vnwitch that which they
haue done?

Dan. Although they deale not directly by the deuill,
I meane they haue no familiar fpirites that fpeake vnto
them yet they deale by deuillifh deuifes, which are alfo an
abhomination to the Lord. For all thofe feuerall fortes of
witches which the Lord rehearfeth, Deut. 18. did not deale
directlie with deuils. For fome were obferuers of times,
which had their luckie dayes and their vnluckie dayes, and
fo their howers. If they goe to buy or to fell, they choofe
their hower to fet foorth in. Some dealt by the intralles of
beafts, and by the flying of birds, by meeting with an hare,
or a foxe, and on which hand, & a thoufand fuch like. Some
deal with the Siue and a paire of fheeres, vfing certaine
words: Some vfe a charme for the tooth ach, another for
the ague, and for ftopping the bleeding at the nofe, alfo
their fpell for the theefe, and a thoufande fuch like, when
butter will not come, when cheefe will not runne, nor Ale
worke in the fatte: Thefe would feeme of all others to haue
witches in the greateft deteftation, and in the meane time
worke by the deuill themfelues, and may bee termed witches.

M. B.

# witches and witchcraftes.

_M._ B. We doe count them witches which haue their spirits, we doe not take them to be witches which doe but vse those things which the cunning men haue taught. For they doe not mean to doe any thing by the deuill. We thinketh therefore it is hard to call them witches.

Dan. Take the name of witchcraft for all that dealeth by the power and deuices of the deuill. No doubt some are more horrible than other of the seuerall sortes of witches, yet the lightest of them be abhominations before the Lord, as we are taught, _Deut._ 18. and the ignorance doeth not excuse. For what though the witch suppose it is the soule of Moses, which appeareth in his Chrystal, is he not therefore a witch? Your neighbour, whose butter wold not come, which heat a spit red hoat and thrust into the creame, vsing certaine wordes, doth thinke she did by the power of God fray away the deuill, is she not therefore a witch, dealing with that which the deuil, and not God hath taught? Is she not a witch also in seeking help at deuils? They which did burne the cloaths which their child lay in, to know by the burning blacke whether it were bewitched, and to bring the witch thither, dealt altogether by the power and direction of the deuill, & so in scratching, for God hath taught no such things, then are they not witches? By whose instruction, and by whose power was the witch fetched home at the burning of the hair of the butchers sonne you spake of? Was not all done by the power of Satan, and by his instruction? Are not they then which practize the thinges the Disciples of witches, & so indeed very witches? Those which haue their charmes, and their night spels, what can they be but witches? I might reckon vp her that dealeth with the siue and the sheares, and a number of such trumperies, in all which the most holie name of God is polluted, and if any thing be done, it is done wholly by the effectuall working of Satan. God hath giuen naturall helps, and those we may vse, as from his hand against naturall

G.                    disea-

diseases,but things besides nature he hath not appointed,
especiallie, they be ridiculous to drive away deuilles and
diseases.

*M.* B. Now you speak of naturall things, we sée there
be great secretes in nature : the Adamant draweth Iron
vnto it. And why m ay there not be some force in these naturall things then?

Dan. No doubt there be great secrets in nature, which
the skilfull Phystians,and naturall Philosophers do find
out.As the hanging of some thinge about the necke, may
haue force to drive away an ague, the wearing of some
thing may haue such vertue to deliuer from the cramp,and
such like. And from these Satan doeth take occasion to
bring in his trumperies,and curious deuiles. As because
there be secretes in nature, a ring is curiouslie framed according to the signes in the firmament, this is tied to a
thread,and let downe into a basen or cup of water,and wil
shew great things.Because there be secretes in nature,
a horshoo must be heat red hot,and then put into a kettle sée-
thing vpon the fire to drive away the witches spirite. Also
he that hath his cattle bewitched,burneth some liue thing,
as hogge or henne,to drive out the deuill. Can these naturall thinges expell deuils? Nay, they play the rancke witches,which burne any thing for to expell deuils: for, hath
God taught to doe anie such thing? Doe they burne the
thing to God,or is it as a verie burnt sacrifice to the Deuill? In the time of the law burnt sacrifices were offred to
God: the deuill among the heathen drewe the like to him-
self:And now by his sleight he doth after some sort procure
the same at their hands, which professe to be Christians,
and thus worshipping him, he ceaseth from hurting their
bodies,or their cattell, as gaining a greater matter.

*M.* B. If it be so(as I am not able to gainsay it)then be
there multitudes in all places which are guiltie of sorce-
rie and witchcraft. For I sée many deale in matters by
the

the help and power of the deuill, which are perswaded o-
therwise. But I meruaile much at diuers things touching
the help which men haue by deuils. Let vs conferre a little
about them. The deuill doeth know things past, & things
present, but God onelie doth know what shall bee done in
the time to come. If these cunning men doe deale with no
further power, than the power of the deuill, howe can they
tell so right what shall come to passe?

Dan. It is peculiar to God alone, to know what shall
come to passe hereafter. But the Lord God hath reuealed
by his Prophetes, and Apostles many thinges that after
should be fulfilled. Satan can giue a nere coniecture when
these come to be fulfilled. Hee is a most subtill obseruer of
thinges, and will gesse at many: but especially, where hee
hath power giuen him to worke and to bring any matter
about, he can and will tell it aforehand. Finally, God in his
iust iudgement giueth him power to seduce the wicked.

M. B. I pray you open your meaning more fully.

Dan. Uery well: In which haue you any doubt?

M. B. I take it the Deuill gesseth at things which are
prophecied, and is a sharpe obseruer of causes. But you
said he telleth what shall be where he worketh that which
he foretelleth: giue some example for this.

Dan. There needeth no better example, than that
which you tolde of the Churchwardens that went to the
cunning man, to knowe the theefe which had stollen their
communion cuppe. It may be sayd, where the cunning
man bad them go to such a place, such a night, and at such
an hower, and thither shall come he that stole the cup, how
could the deuill tell, if it were a night or two after, that he
should come to that place, and at that hower? You muste
note what power the deuill hath in the mind of a theefe. He
stirred him vp to steale the cup. He stirred vp the Churchwardens to seeke to the cunning witch. Hee nameth the
place and the time, whether, and when he would: moue the

heart

heart of the théefe to come: And at the time appointed hée
bꝛingeth him thither, foꝛ he that coulo moue him to ſteale,
coulo alſo by ſecrete ſuggeſtion mooue him to goe thither.
The deuill tolo that the witch ſhulo come home with ſpéo
that hao bewitched the butchers ſon: he that hao power in
her heart to make her become a witch, oio know he ſhoulo
haue power to make her with haſte to come home. One carieth ſomewhat which a ſick perſon hath lien in to the cunning man. he can tell, it ſéemeth, by the ſmell of the cloth,
whether the deuil hath bene in it (if it ſmell like his deuill)
ano ſo telleth, the partie is bewitched. Take the clothes
which the ſicke partie hath lien in, ano burne them, if they
burne blacke, then may you ſée it is ſo, ano the witch ſhall
come in while they be a burning. Nowe, if the Loꝛo gaue
him power, ano he hath ſtriken ano toꝛmented the bodie of
the ſicke perſon: ano if hee haue collourably ſtirred vp a
witch to ſeno him: Is it not an eaſie matter foꝛ him to
make the fire burne blacke, ano to mooue the witch to
come at that pꝛeſent? Oꝛ if he haue power foꝛ to toꝛment,
ano hath no witch to ſeno him, his great deſire being to
haue men guiltie of innocent bloon, is it not as eaſie by the
permiſſion of Goo, which in his iuſt iuogment, giueth him
power to ſeduce ſuch people as will hearken vnto deuils,
foꝛ him to make the fire burne blacke, oꝛ at leaſt to ſéeme ſo
to them, ano to mooue ſome frowaroe ſuſpected woman
oꝛ other to come in, though ſhe be no witch? A thouſande
ſuch things hee woꝛketh in, ano as a cunning iuggler can
compaſſe ano bꝛing them about.

M. B. Inoéo an innocent perſon may come in at ſuch
a time: but I haue heard, I cannot tell howe true it is, that
therefoꝛe there is a further thing which they obſerue. Ano
that is this, the cunning man biooeth, ſet on a poſnet oꝛ
ſome pan with nayles, ano ſéeth them, ano the witch ſhal
come in while they be in ſéething, ano within a fewe oayes
after, her face will be all beſcratched with the nailes. Ano

1

I haue heard that some olde woman comming in, her face hath indeed bene as it were scratched within a few dayes after, for the shingles or such like breake forth.

Dan. O the depth of Satans illusions to make blinde people becom witches, and to deale by him. He doth know the corrupted humours in the bodie, which will breake out into the smal pockes, or such like, and if he can procure one to come in which is euen ready to haue them, what a shew doth he make, as if the nails did it?

M. B. This were great subtiltie of Satan.

Dan. Nay, we are not able to imagine the depth of his sleights, neither can we sée the secrete force, wherwith he moueth the minds of ignorant people, and so bringeth about his enterprises. There doth lie the greatest cunning of Satan.

M. B. Indéed it séemeth strange and vncredible that the deuil should so moue the minds of men, and lead them vnto this thing and that thing, and in the meane time they doe not know it, but thinke they goe against the deuil. But now I haue a further doubt. I confesse it is an easie thing for the deuill to tell where a thing is that is lost or stollen, but what power hath he to heale that which is sick or sore? Out of question they be innumerable which receiue helpe by going to the cunning men. You say he helpeth the bodie that he may destroy the soule. Hee helpeth that men may séeke vnto him, and so set him, as it were, in the place of God. He thinketh it should not be in the power of deuilles for to helpe.

Dan. Indeed that is well mooued, there lieth a great sleight of the deuill in it. You say that innumerable do receiue help by going vnto cunning men. I warrant you not so many as you are perswaded.

M. B. O verie manie. There be a number which doe neuer make it knowne, because it is misliked by some.

Dan. Yea, and there be many which come home again

with

with a flea in their eare, they receiue an answere, as good
as a flim flam.

M. B. It may be they come too late, the matter is ouer
farre spent, and if they had come sooner, they coulde haue
holpen them.

Dan. Yea, a number of such cosoning answers the deuill maketh which satisfie ignorant people, which are rea-
to beleue all that he telleth, and to daunce after his pipe.
One commeth to him for his childe, if he know the disease
be deadly, he will say it is bewitched, but so farre spent,
that there is no help, the childe wil hardlie liue two daies:
the father commeth home and findeth his child deade, or it
dieth within two or three dayes after, here the deuill get-
teth credit. Another is sicke and grieuously tormented, hee
sendeth: Satan doth see (for he sendeth them) that the disease is euen spent, and that the cause of it begin to fail, and
so that the partie in a few dayes will recouer, here he pre-
scribeth one paltrie or other, they vse it, the man is recouered, and so should haue bene without the deuils medicine,
but now Satan hath gotten further credite. Another is
sicke and languisheth, his neighbours tell him, he may be
bewitched, it is good to send, and then he shal know. He sendeth, the deuill doth not know whether the sicke man can
escape and recouer, or not. He saith, it is like he is bewitched: and teacheth what to doe, if there bee any help at all,
but doubteth, and so whether the man liue or die, Satan
saueth his credite whole and sound. And many of these an-
sweres he giueth. Againe, we must note that mans imagination is of great force, either to continue a disease, or to
diminish and take away some diseases. And in this also
Satan deludeth some, for his medicine seemeth to do somwhat, when it is but the parties conceit.

M. B. These be sleightes indeede: but mee thinketh
you goe farre in the last. I doe not see how a mans conceit
can help him.

Dan.

Dan. Imagination is a strong thing to hurt, all men doe finde, and why should it not then be strong also to help, when the parties mind is cleared, by beleeuing fully that he receiueth ease?

M. B. But yet it is hard to shewe that euer anie such cure hath bene wrought.

Dan. It is not hard to shew, for that which men doe, it is presumed the deuill can doe the like. And I haue heard of a mery companion that wrought such a cure. Ther was one in London (as report goeth) which was acquainted with Feats. Now, this Feats had a blacke dogge, whome he called Bomelius. This partie afterward had a conceit that Bomelius was a deuill, and that hee felt him within him. He was in heauinesse, and made his moane to one of his acquaintance, who had a merie head, he tolde him, he had a friend could remoue Bomelius. Hee bad him prepare a breakfast, and he would bring him. Then this was the cure, he made him be stripped naked and stand by a good fire, and though he were fatte ynough of himselfe, basted him all ouer with butter against the fire, and made him weare a sleeke stone next his skin vnder his bellie, and the man had present remedie, and gaue him afterward greate thankes.

M. B. I know men haue many foolish imaginations: but though one imagination may driue out another, which is not the curing of any disease in deed, but of an imagination: yet it doth not followe, that where there is an apparant griefe, that a mans conceit can helpe to cure it.

Dan. Yes, the conceit doth much, euen where there is an apparant disease. A man feareth hee is bewitched, it troubleth al the powers of his mind, and that distempereth his bodie, maketh great alterations in it, and bringeth sundrie griefes. Now, when his minde is freed from such imaginations, his bodily griefe which grew from the same is eased. And a multitude of Satans cures are but such.

M. B.

*M. B.* Nay, there be also euils which be apparant in the bodie, and bee cured., which come not of anie feare or imagination: how can these be cured by any conceit? There is great reason that such griefes may be cured indeede by quieting the minde, as did growe from the disturbance of the same.

*Dan.* Yea, and that falleth out sometimes in griefes of the body, which doeth not growe from imagination, but from some other passions. As I can giue you an example, which is written and reported by a very reuerend learned Physitian. The cure was done by a lewde cosening knaue in Germanie. A woman had bleare eies that were watery. The knaue lodging there, promised for certainty that hee would heale them: hee did hang a litle writing about her necke, charging strictlie, that it should not be taken from thence nor read, nor opened, for if any of these were done, she could haue no help at all by it. The woman had such a confidence in the thinge, and was so merry and glad, that she left weeping (for her often weeping and teares had spoiled her eies) and so by little and litle, the moysture stayed, and her eies were whole. It fell out that she lost the writing, whereat she was in such griefe and sorrowe, and weeping, that her eies were sore againe. Another founde the writing, opened it, and read it. It was written in the Germane tongue, to this effect translated into English: The deuill pluck out thine eies, and fill their holes with his dung. Was not this, thinke you, a proper salue for to cure her eies? If this medicine had taken effect, her eies shuld not haue ben healed, but plucked quite out. We may not think but that Satan hath mo cosening tricks than al men in the world, for men are but his schollers. Againe, where men faile, he can worke somewhat in the affections of the parties mindes. And you shall heare them say, when any charme is vsed, you must beleeue it will helpe, or els it will doe you no good at all. Thus if it were well seene into,

the

the greateſt part of your innumerable cures, come to bee mere coſonages.

*M. B.* Well, let all this be true as you haue ſaide: Yet there be many thinges wherein the deuilles doe helpe. What ſay you to the boy which healed within few daies af-he had ſcratched the witch, whereas his ſores were moſt grieuous before, and could not be cured? What ſay you to that which they doe, when butter will not come, or when drinke will not worke in the fat? What ſay you to the bur-ning of ſome liue thing, as hogge or henne, and the harme ceaſſing? And finallie, what ſay you to the helping of them where the deuill is, and doth torment their bodies?

*Dan.* All theſe are anſwered in few wordes, that where he hath power to hurt either man or beaſt, drinke or butter he helpeth only by giuing place, and ceaſing to hurt, which as I ſhewed you before, he doth moſt willinglie, to bring to paſſe, that men may ſeek to him, & become euen verie wit-ches. If a man be vexed & tormented by a deuil, & men ſeek by faſting & prayer to caſt him forth, euen inſtantly intrea-ting the Lord, then he goeth out with much a do, and vnwil-lingly, as ouercome & expelled by the power of God. But when he hurteth, as you ſay he did the butchers ſonne, and they ſeeke to him, and will followe his preſciptions, as to draw blood of the witch, he goeth out willingly, I meane he ceaſeth from hurting the bodie: for he goeth not out in-deede, but rather goeth further in, and ſeateth himſelfe dee-per in the ſoule. And ſo is it in all the reſt. How gladlie wil he ceaſe to hurte the hennes, ſo that to pleaſe him, a henne may be burnt aliue: his helping is no more but a ceaſing from doing harme, if he had power giuen him to hurt.

*Sam.* This is a ſtrange thing if it be ſo. There be thou-ſands in the land deceiued. The woman at R. H. by report hath ſome weeke fourtie come vnto her, and many of them not of the meaner ſort. But I doe but hinder, I pray you go forward.

H           *Dan.*

Dan. The deuill can deceiue thousand thousands, and euen the wisest for this world, when they will not be taught of God, but dispise his doctrine, then are they iustly giuen ouer to be disciples of the deuill.

M. B. If there be such deceit in all these things, and that the witches do not kill nor hurt, but the deuill craftilie séemeth to kill and to hurt when the diseases be naturall and maketh the witch beleeue that hee hath done all at her request. Or where God hath giuen him power, he stirreth her vp to send him, as if either hee could not, or would not meddle, vnles he had bene sent. Seeing all lieth vpon Satan, it should seeme, there is no reason that witches should be put to death: but the scripture doth command they shuld be put to death.

Dan. The holy scriptures doe command that witches should be put to death: therein you say right: but if you did take it, that the word of God commaundeth they shall not be suffered to liue, because they kill men and beastes, or because they send their spirits which possesse men, and torment their bodies, you are much deceiued: For you shal neuer finde, of all that haue bene tormented and plagued by euill spirites, that the holie Ghoste layeth it vpon witches. The causes why they should be put to death are, that they haue familiaritie with deuils, which are the blasphemous enemies of God: and that they seduce the people into error, to runne after deuils, and deuilish practises, and that they haue such wicked minds. Although they neuer minde to kill or to hurt any, but to doe them good, as they imagine, yet if they deale with deuilles they ought to die for it.

M. B. Then you take it, that these cunning men and women, vnto whome so many runne for helpe, which are thought to do very much good, and no hurt at all, ought to be rooted out, and destroyed. Let vs knowe what scripture there is for it.

Dan.

Dan. Yea, of all other they ought to die, because they doe the greatest harme. Other witches that haue spirites are thought to doe harm, because the deuil at the appointment of God doth harme, and he beareth in hand hee doeth it at the request of the witch: but these that seeme to doe good, do harme indeed, and that many wayes, as euerie one that light in him, may easily see. And for the scripture s which shewe that they ought to die, reade first in the 22. chapter of Exodus. ver. 18. and there it is said, Thou shalt not suffer a witch to liue.

M. B. That place we take to be meant of these witches which send their spirits to doe harme: the other be not called witches.

Dan. It is that witch that is there commanded to be put to death, that is called Mecasshephah: such were they and so called, which before Pharaoh did withstand Moses, and made in shewe rods turned into serpents. So that in one kinde the Lord doeth include all such as worke by the deuill. For there be diuers others sortes named in Deut. 18. and they bee all called an abhomination to the Lorde: and no abhomination is to be suffered to remaine among the Lords people. Also in the same place, when he saith, Let there not be found in thee any such or such, as he there reckoneth them vp: It is not alone to will that none should practize such thinges, but also that they should bee rooted out.

M. B. I must needs agree vnto that which the worde of God doth set down. But this is the hardest matter of al, how they shall be conuicted.

Dan. Why doe you take it to bee the hardest matter, how a witch shall be conuicted? how is a theefe or a murtherer conuicted but by proofe? If there be vehement suspition, and the party vpon examination confesse the fact, that is a sufficient proofe. If the partie doe denie, and two or three of credite doe testifie vpon their knowledge with a so-

H 2                                      lemne

# A Dialogue concerning

lemne oath, that he is guiltie of the fact, that is also a sufficient proofe. And touching this, God commanded by Moses, that none should dy, vnlesse the matter were proued
against them by two witnesses at the least. Deutronom.
19.ver.15.

*M. B.* I graunt, if the partie do denie, and especially,
if the matter touch life, that there ought by the worde of
God to be due proofe by two witnesses at the least. This
may be for murtherers, this may be for theeues: but for
witches I see not how. They deale so secretely with their
spirits, that very seldome they can be conuinced by flat te-
stimonies of men, as to say directly they haue heard or seen
them send their spirits. And againe, it is a rare thinge to
haue a witch confesse. For it is generallie thought the deuill hath such power ouer them, that he wil not suffer them
to confesse.

*Dan.* O then I perceiue why you account it the hardest
matter of all to conuict a witch, if both testimony and confession doe fayle: but what would you haue further?

*M. B.* I haue bene of this opinion, that if there were
any likelihood, and suspition, and common fame, that it
was euen proofe ynough, and the best deede that could be
done for to hang them vp, and so to ridde the countrey of
them

*Dan.* Then you thought that their spirites were hanged with them, and so the country being rid of the witches
and their spirits, mens bodies and their cattell should bee
safe.

*M. B.* I had a little more wit than to thinke so: but in
trueth it was but a litle more. For I thought if all the witches were hanged, that then their spirits shoulde not haue
anie to hire them, nor to send them to hurte eyther man or
beaste, but I see mine owne follie, and that onlie God giueth the power vnto the deuils to afflict and trie the godly,
and to vexe, torment, and plague the wicked, and that they
                                                        shall

# witches and witchcraftes.

shall do this, though all the witches in the world were hanged. I know they néede none to cherish them, or to set them
a worke.

Dan. But did you not feare if all suspected should be
hanged, then some guiltles persons might be put to death?
As you sée manie that haue bene executed as witches haue
taken it vpon their death that they were innocent.

M. B. I will tel you my thought touching that point,
which was this. The witches raise tempestes, and hurte
corne and fruites vpon the trées, the witches bring the pe-
stilence among men, and murraine among cattell: the witches send their spirits and make men lame, kill their children and their cattell: their spirits cannot bee taken héede
of, nor kept out with doores and wals as théeues and murtherers, but come in when they bee sent, and doe so many
harmes: for this cause I thought it a marueilous good
worke to put all suspected to death, though some of them
were innocent, that so sure worke might be made to haue
not one left.

Dan. Did you not thinke it a fearfull thinge to shead
innocent blood.

M. B. Yea, but I thought it much better that some
should be put to death wrongfully, than to leaue any one
witch, which might kill and destroy many.

Dan. Then I perceiue that this was the reason which
did perswade you, that it was very good to put all to death
that were suspected (although it might fall out that some
of them were innocent) to auoyde greater inconuenience,
and that is, if some few witches should escape, which might
plague and kill many. Better a few should be put wrongfully to death, then many should bee tormented and killed,
or lamed by the deuilles. But are you still of that mind?

M. B. No verily. For you haue put me in minde that
the wicked spirits receiue their power to plague both men
and beasts, only from God. They séeke about, they watch

P 3                                                        when

when and where hee will giue them leaue to touch, where God will trie the faith and patience of the iust by him, as he did in Iob, he sendeth him, if he will be sent by a witch, it is but vnder a collour, shee giueth him not the power, hee would touch though shee were not. Where God will strike and plague the wicked by him, he giueth him leaue, it is not the anger of the witch that bringeth it, but their owne wickednes, whereby they haue prouoked God to displeasure, and so giue this enemy power ouer them.

Dan. Then so long as these two thinges stand, that God by Satan will afflict in some sort and trie his children(as you alleage he did Iob) and that he will vse him as his executioner, to plague and torment the wicked, as he sent an euill spirite to vexe king Saule : so long the harmes done by wicked spirites shall not cease, although all the witches and coniurers in the worlde were hanged vp. Looke then to the causes, if wee will remooue the effects. As if thou feare God, and Satan afflict thee, stand fast in faith and patience, and waite vpon God for thy deliuerance. If thou endure temptation, thou art blessed, and shalt be crowned. Iam. 1. ver. 12. If thy sinnes haue prouoked God, and the enemie doth touch thy body or thy goods, fall downe and humble thy selfe with fasting and prayer, intreat the Lord to turne away his displeasure: looke not vpon the witch, lay not the cause where it is not, seeke not help at the hands of deuils, be not a disciple of witches, to commit thinges abhominable, by polluting the name of God, and honouring Satan, nor thirst not after the blood which is innocent, as it falleth out in many.

M. B. I doe assent vnto al this : and surely it is a great fault to shead innocent blood.

Dan. We may learne in the holie scriptures, that the sheading of innocent blood is a verie horrible thing in the eies of almightie God: and a very grieuous thing it is to haue a land polluted with innocent blood: and that is one
speciall

special cause why Satan dealeth by witches: for he laboureth to wrappe in many guiltlesse persons vpon suspitions, he suggesteth by his helping witches, that ther be many hurting witches in all townes, and villages, that so hee may set the multitude in a rage, and to suspect vpon euery likelihood that he can deuise or make shewe of. And thus whole Iuries must become guiltie of innocent blood, by condemning as guiltie, and that vpon their solemne oath, such as be suspected vpon vaine surmises and imaginations, and illusions, rising from blindnes and infidelitie, and feare of Satan which is in the ignorant sort.

*M. B.* If you take it, that this is one craft of Satan, to bring manie to be guiltie of innocent blood, and euen vpon their oathes, which is horrible, what wold you haue the iudges and Iuries to doe, when any are arraigned of suspition to be witches?

Dan. What would I haue them doe? I would with them to bee most warie and circumspect that they bee not guilty of innocent blood. And that is, to condemne none but vpon sure ground, and infallible proofs, because presumptions shall not warrant or excuse them before God if guiltlesse blood be shead.

*M. B.* It falleth out sometimes when a theefe is arraigned, or a murtherer, that direct euidence faileth, and yet such circumstances are brought, as doe euen enforce the Iurie in their conscience to find them guiltie: It seemeth that this holdeth chiefly about witches, because their dealing is close and secrete, and it is also thought that the deuill hath so great power ouer them, that he will not suffer them to confesse.

Dan. You bring two reasons to prooue that in conuicting witches, likelihoods and presumptions ought to be of force more than about theues or murtherers: The first, because their dealing is secrete: the other because the deuill will not let them confesse. Indeede men imagining that

witches do worke strange mischiefes, burne in desire to
haue them hanged, as hoping then to be frée, and then vpon
such perswasions as you mention, they suppose it is a very
good worke to put to death all which are suspected. But
touching theeues and murtherers let men take héede how
they deale vpon presumptions, vnles they be very stron g
for we sée that Iuries sometimes doe condemne such as be
guiltlesse, which is an hard thing, especiallie being vpon
their oath. And in witches aboue all other, the proofe s had
néed to be strong: because there is greater sleight of Satan
to pursue the guiltles vnto death, than in the other. Here
is speciall care and wisdome to be vsed. And so likewise for
their confessing, Satan doth gaine more by their confession, than by their deniall, and therefore rather bewrayeth
them himselfe, and forceth them to confession, oftener than
vnto deniall.

    *M.* B. These things are beyond my reach, I cannot
conceiue of them. I pray you open it so as that I may perceiue your meaning, and sée some ground of reason for that
which you shall affirme.

    Dan. Then is it requisite to stande vpon them more
at large. And let vs begin with the latter.

    M. B. If you go first to the latter, then shew some rea-
son or experience that Satan bewrayeth the witches, and
draweth them to confesse, and to disclose themselues, rather
than to conceale and hide their doings. I can tell you this
before hand, that the common opinion is otherwise, which
séemeth to be grounded both vpon reason and experience.

    Dan. I know the common opinion is as you say: But
I do much marueill at it, séeing reason and experience doe
proue the contrary as I will shew. As first, touching reason, you will grant, that the deuils dealing altogether by
sleight and subtilties, doe that which doeth most further
their purposes and desires.

    *M.* B. That is the verie reason why the deuill would
by

by no meanes haue the witches bewrayed, as it is thought
becausehe would lurke secretely to doe mischiefe.

Dan. Indeed it were a good reason to proue that part,
if Satan receiued his power from the witch, or could doe
nothing but by her sending, or næded to be harboured by
her, or had no minde to meddle, but as it were hired to sa=
tiffie her wrath. But seeing al these be absurd, and he vseth
the witch and coniurer but vnder a colour to bring in fur=
ther euils, it must needs followe, that the disclosing is fit=
ter for his purpose, than the keeping secrete, for if they
should be kept secrete, how should he make men think that
he doth so many harmes at the request of the witch? howe
should he drawe so many to runne after deuils, to seek help
at their handes? how should he procure so many to vse wic=
ked and blasphemous charms and sorceries, and in so hor=
rible maner to abuse the blessed name of God, and his most
sacred word? Or how should he draw the people into ma=
nifold errours, and to thirst euen in rage after innocent
blood? All these and a number such like hee procureth and
furthereth, by disclosing witches.

M. B. But how shall this reason be confirmed by ex=
perience: No doubt in shew he is loath to haue his Dame
(as some speake) disclosed.

Dan. You say well, that in shew he is loath to haue the
witch bewrayed: for indæde it is onely in shewe, sæing hee
would make her and others also beléue, euen when he doth
bewray her by one means or other, that it is sore against
his liking.

M. B. I pray you make that euident.

Dan. When one féeleth himselfe plagued any way, and
doeth take it to be by Satan, admit it be so: he goeth to a
cunning man, and he sheweth him in a glasse, or in a Chry=
stall the shape of the witch. Who now bewrayeth her?

M. B. That is the cunning mans spirite which be=
wrayeth her, and not her spirit which she dealeth withall.

I                    Dan.

Dan. You are not sure of that : for it may be the same deuill that she dealeth withall, that resembleth her in the glasse: none can doe it better.

M. B. I doe not thinke that he departeth away from her.

Dan. Yea, but you must remember that she which dealeth with a spirit, dealeth not with a deuill, but with deuils : for manie doe ioyn together. When one of them departeth and carieth the matter to the cunning man, they do not all depart. But what if it be as you said, that som other spirits do bewray, doe you thinke he doeth it against the liking of the witches spirite? Is Satan deuided against Satan? Will Satan bewray Satan to his hindrance? Remember what our Sauiour hath taught touching that.

M. B. Then if it be so, doe you not take it a sufficient proofe against a witch, euen for a Iurie to finde guilty vpon their oath, if a cunning man by his spirite doe bewray anie.

Dan. It is the most insufficient proofe that can bee, for although he doe tell true in bewraying many, as their own cofessions do witnes: yet he doeth it of an euill purpose, he is a lyer, and the father of lies, he desireth chiefly to accuse the innocent, that he may bring men to bee guilty of innocent blood, to make the people beleeue there be multitudes of witches, to set them a work to learne charmes and sorceries, and chiefly, that they may be brought to seeke vnto him, as the bewrayer euen in pitie, of such bad people. Now, because he craftily bewrayeth some, to get credite, shall mens verdict by oath, euen vnto blood, be grounded vpon his testimony? If a deuill should come in vnto a Iurie, and say the partie about whome you enquire is a witch, should they beleeue him, or wold they say let him be sworn, and witnesse vpon his oath? If not, why should they beleeue that which he hath spoken to the cunning man?

M. B. Surely I am out of doubt he doth all in craft

vnto

vnto a most bad purpose, and that no credite ought to bee giuen vnto his testimony when it is voluntary. But what say you to his testimonie, when he is euen charged and forced in the name and power of God to tell the trueth? It seemeth then he would conceale, but cannot.

*Dan.* The coniurer which supposeth that hee dooth bind by the name and power of God to tell him the trueth, is vtterlie deluded. For he is not bound, but is glad that the most glorious name of God is so horriblie abused, and that hee can drawe men into such a gulfe of all abhomination.

*M. B.* Nay, I doe not meane the coniurer, but when such as be godlie go about to cast him foorth by prayer.

*Dan.* This I take to bee your meaning, a man or a woman is possessed with a Deuill, put case it bee so indæde (to distinguish them from so many counterfaits, as haue bene) and men assemble together where the possessed is, and cald vpon God, and then charge Satan in the name of Christ to tell how hee came there, and who sent him.

*M. B.* I meane so indæde. And some being possessed, the deuill being charged to tell who sent him, he hath confessed, that such a man did coniure him in thither, or such a witch did send him. Shall not this be of force to conuince?

*Dan.* When any is possessed by the fiend, mens compassion, their loue and pity are to be shewed, euen to helpe what they can in such a distresse. They ought with all instant suit to intreat the Lord to shew mercy, and to expell him. The doctrin of the holy scriptures doth warrant this: but for men to talke and question with him, I sæ no warrant at all by Gods word, much lesse to commaund and adiure him to depart. He is the Lords executioner, he hath sent him, wee may intreat the Lord to remoue him, but what authority haue we to command him to depart, where God hath sent him?

*M. B.* Men haue no authority, I grant, but they com-

I 2　　　　　　mand

mand and adiure him in the name and power of the Lord, for to depart.

*Dan.* That I take ought not to be, for mark this comparison: the Prince is displeased with a subiect for some disloyaltie : An Officer is sent from the Prince to attach and imprison him: shall he or any other charge this Officer in the Princes name to let him alone, and not to meddle ? Is not their way only to pacifie the Prince, and so the Prince will command the Officer to cease? Euen so, wher God sendeth Satan his executioner, the only way is to intreat the Lord to be pacified, for then shall the tormentor no longer remaine.

*M. B.* Howe doeth this which you speake agrée with that which we read in the Acts of the Apostles, howe S. Paule commaunded the deuill to come out of a Mayde at Philippos?

*Dan.* The holy Apostles and others in the Primitiue Church, had an extraordinary power giuen them to caste foorth deuils, and to heale diseases, and they did execute the same power by the direction and instinct of the holy Ghost: We may not draw a patterne from that.

*M.B.* We sée that deuils are sometimes expelled.

*Dan.* They are when the Lord is intreated, otherwise they but séeme to be bound by adiuration and expelled. But how can it be prooued, that the father of lies may be bound, and forced through charge and adiuration in the name and power of God to tell the trueth ? And what warrant haue we to learne any trueth from his mouth ? As to say we command thée in the name of God, that thou tel vs who sent thée. Who sent thée? who sent thée ? Mother Joan, Mother Joan, saith he : Also we command thée to tell vs, who sent thée. L. B. coniured me in hither (saith he) Shal wee thinke he doeth this euen compelled ? Or shall we ground vpon it for certaintie, that he telleth no lie?

*M. B.* The deuill in a partie possessed hath said, such a

man

man coniured me in hither. The coniurer hath bene put
to death for it, and hath confessed so much. The deuill in an
other hath said, such a woman sent me; it hath likewise bene
confessed by the woman.

Dan. All this maketh for that which I affirme. The
Lord giueth him power to possesse a man. He vnder a collour will be sent by a coniurer, or by a witch: and the one
thinketh the deuill entreth at her intreaty: the other supposeth he doeth euen bind him thereto, whereas he ruleth both
their mindes, and setteth them a worke. Then doeth hee
willingly bewray them, euen for many subtill purposes:
but chiefly, that he may establish coniurations, witchcrafts
and charmes, that he may be sought vnto, that he may set
the people a worke in their calamities to be troubled about
witches and coniurers, as though they could plague, and
neuer looke to God, and that bewraying some witches and
coniurers, he may winne credite, and be beleeued, euen
when he accuseth falslie, that he may bring innocent blood
vpon the land. Let all men take heed how vpon their oath
they giue a verdict, especially touching life, vpon his word
howsoeuer he seeme to be forced thereunto: all is most deepe
craft and subtilty in him.

Sam. I pray you giue me leaue to speake a litle. You
say the deuill willinglie bewrayeth witches and coniurers
and that for many subtill purposes. I haue heard of diuers
things done of late which seeme quite contrarie, and that
he taketh it grieuously when they doe confesse and bewray
matters.

Dan. He will seeme to take it in euill part, but let vs
heare the matters, and you shall see plainely that hee iug-
gleth, and maketh shewe of that which is contrary to his
practise.

Sam. Well, I haue heard very credibly, that a woman
of late, suspected another woman to be a witch, & that she
had hurt her some way. She procured a gentleman to send

for the partie suspected, and charging her in his presence,
she left her to the Gentleman, who taking her aside, and
walking alone with her, began to admonish and perswade
her to renounce the deuill & to forsake such wicked waies:
While he was thus perswading, and she denying stiffely
that she was any such woman, suddainly there appeared
some distance from them, a Weasill or Lobsterre looking
euen vpon them. Looke (said the Gentleman)yonder same
is thy spirit. Ah maister(said she)that is a vermine, there
be many of them euery where. Well, as they went towards
it, it was vanished out of sight: by and by it appeared a-
gaine, and looked vpon them. Surely (saide the Gentleman)it is thy spirit:but she still denyed, and with that her
mouth was drawne awrie. Then hee pressed her further,
and she confessed all. She confessed shee had hurt and killed by sending her spirit. The Gentleman being no Iustice, let her goe home, and did minde to open the matter
vnto some Iustice: When she was come home, another
witch meeteth her, and saith, Ah thou beast, what hast thou
done:thou hast bewrayed vs all. What remedy nowe(saide
she:) What remedy said the other? send thy spirite & touch
him: she sent her spirit, and of a suddain the Gentleman
had as it wer a flash of fire about him, He lifted vp his hart
to God, and felt no hurt. The spirite returneth, and tolde
he could not hurt him because he had faith: what then, said
the other witch, hath hee nothing that thou maist touch? he
hath a child said the other. Send thy spirit, sayd she, and
touch the child:she sent her spirite, the childe was in great
paine and died. The witches were hanged and confessed.

    Dan. What is the chiefe thing which you alleadge
this for?

    Sam. To shew how vnwilling the deuill was that the
witch should confesse and bewray things No doubt it shuld
séeme, that when the Gentleman was talking with her, hee
appeared to call her away, for fear least she should confesse:

and

and when ſhe would not come away, he drew her mouth a-
wry: and when ſhe had confeſſed, the deuill complayned vnto the other witch, and made her chide her.

Dan. The thing is as clear as may be, that he willinglie bewrayed them : and will you imagine the contrarie?
Why did he appeare in a likeneſſe, but euen to enforce her
for to confeſſe, both by abaſhing, and giuing the Gentleman euident notice, eſpecially, when he drew her mouth a-
wrie? And why did he ſet on the other witch to mooue her
that had confeſſed to ſend her ſpirit, but that he would haue
the matter more open, and bring them both to light.

Sam. What ſhould mooue him to bewray the witches?
what could he gaine by it?

Dan. Nay, what almoſt doth he not gaine by it? Now
all the country ringes of the matter. As if the witches ſet
on their ſpirites to lame and to kill: and that they doe not
meddle, but ſent by them. He did knowe what power he had
from God to afflict any: he will deale by witches: he maketh others affraid of them, that ſo they may accuſe them.
He findeth meanes to haue all diſcloſed. Hee mooueth the
witches to ſend him againſt the gentleman: hee knoweth
what he can doe: he returneth and ſaith there is faith: As
though God did not giue him power ſometimes to afflict
the faithfull? Or as if he could touch al that haue no faith?
If he could, the greateſt part of the world ſhuld be deſtroi-
ed by him. For they be very few in the world in compariſon
which haue the true faith. Then muſt he be ſent to the child
that hath no faith: doeth not the faith of the parents holde
Gods protection ouer their infants as ouer themſelues?
here is Satans craft: either he did know by thinges bree-
ding in the bodie of the child that it would at ſuch time fall
ſicke and die: and he would be taken to bee the killer of the
childe, to beare in hand that he hath ſuch power & wil doe
when he is requeſted. Or els he had power giuen him of
God, and wold bring it about this way. If he did ſtrike the

I 4                                                    childe

childe, do you imagine he doeth it at her pleasure? Or doe
you thinke he would neuer haue thought of any such thing,
but moued by her? Doe not all the armies of deuils goe a-
bout continuallie, seeking whom they may deuour? Do they
not waite where God wil giue them power to strike? Shall
we still be so simple as to thinke that women neede to hire
or to intreat them to doe harme? Looke vnto God, for those
wicked spirits play all parts in the play, and delude both
the witches and others.

Sam. I will tell you another thing which was done of
late. A woman being suspected to be a witch, and to haue
done some hurt among cattell, was examined, and confessed indæd, that she had a spirite which did abide in a hollow
træ, where there was an hole, out of which hee spake vnto
her. And euer when she was offended with anie, shee went
to that træ, and sent him to kill their cattell. She was perswaded to confesse her fault openly, and to promise that she
wold vtterly forsak such vngodly waies: after she had made
this open confession, the spirite came vnto her being alone.
Ah, said he, thou hast confessed and bewrayed all, I coulde
tære it to rend thæ in pæces: with that she was affrayde,
and wound away, and got her into company. Within some
few weeks after, she fel out greatly into anger against one
man. Towards the træ she goeth, and before she came at it,
Ah, said the spirite, wherefore commest thou? who hath angred thæ? Such a man, said the witch. And what wouldest
thou haue me doe saide the spirite? He hath (saith she) two
horses going yonder, touch them or one of them. Well, I
thinke euen that night one of the horses died, and the other
was litle better. Indæde they recouered that one againe
which was not dead, but in verie euill case. Here mee thinketh it is plaine: he was angry that she had bewrayed all.
And yet when she came to the træ he let goe all displeasure
and went readily.

Dan. Doe you thinke all is plaine here. Indæde here
is

is that plaine dealing which deuils doe vse. First, doe you thinke Satan lodgeth in an hollow treé? Is heé become so lazy, and idle: hath he left off to be as a roaring lion, seéking whome he may deuour? hath he put off the bloody and cru-ell nature of the fiery Dragon, so that he mindeth no harm, but when an angrie woman shall intreat him to goe kill a Cow or a horse: Is he become so doting with age, that men shall espie his craft: yea, be found craftier than he is? Alas may there not be deép subtiltie in these things?

*Sam.* Doe you thinke there is nothiug but subtiltie in these thmgs?

*Dan.* Doe I think there is nothing but subtiltie? Tel me what you thinke. What other end can there be but sub-tiltie?

*Sam.* He may haue this purpose (as I think the deuils studie nothing els) to do harme.

*Dan.* I doe not denie that: for all his craft tendeth vn-to harme. But what harme meane you?

*Sam.* You seé here he killed mens cattel.

*Dan.* It may be he did: but how know you that?

*Sam.* You seé he went at her request & killed one horse, and almost killed the other.

*Dan.* I wold be loath to aduenture my hand vpon that: For who told you, that he killed the one, and almost killed the other?

*Sam.* The witch her selfe hath confessed the whole matter.

*Dan.* Who told the witch so?

*Sam.* Her spirit told her that he did it at her request.

*Dan.* He is a credible person, and kind heé was vnto her as it seémeth.

*Sam.* Nay, but we see all things fell out according as she confessed.

*Dan.* How doe you meane?

*Sam.* Why, she confessed her fault, the spirite was an-

K

grie

grie with her, afterward she fell out with that man, and vpon this his horse died, she confessed she sent the spirit, how
could all things fall out so fit?

Dan. The spirite when she came towardes the trée, as-
ked her, wherfore commest thou? who hath angred thée?

Sam. He did so.

Dan. And doe you imagine that the deuill did lie there
and knew nothing vntill she came and told him?

Sam. Why néeded he to aske her if he did know?

Dan. Because hee is subtill: for hee wrought in her
heart, and kindled her wrath, and procured the falling
out betweene her and that man: he did knowe eyther that
the horses at that time had somwhat in them which would
bring death, or els that the Lord had giuen him power for
to strike them: he moued and wrought in her heart to haue
her come againe to the trée: he séemed to be angrie that she
had cōfessed before, but was not, but sought to haue things
knowne. If he had not knowne that the horse should die,
either by some naturall cause, which woulde then breake
foorth, or by some power giuen to him, he wold not at this
time haue moued her heart to goe to the trée. And if her
wrath had without his suggestion caried her so farre, he
could quickly haue turned her: for great is the efficacie of
Satans working in the hearts of such.

Sam. But I marked one thing which you said before,
as that it might be that God giueth sometimes power to
the Deuill, euen at the sending of the witch.

Dan. I say that God in iustice giueth power vnto
Satan to delude, because men refuse to loue his trueth: but
that maketh not that the deuill obtaineth any power to
hurt because the witch sendeth, but the fault is in men, the
sinnes of the people giue power to the deuill: for God is
offended, and sendeth (as *S.* Paule saith) strong delusi-
on. But haue you any mo examples to prooue that the Deuill is not willing to haue witches betrayed?

Sam.

Sam. I haue heard of many such like, but you say all is but craft, and that he would haue men thinke hee doeth all harmes that are done.

Dan. The Deuill would haue men beleeue that hee doth all, if he could bring it about: And therefore, it is for his aduantage if he doe hurte, to haue it not kept secrete, but openly to be made knowne.

M. B. what say you then vnto this, a witch is apprehended vpon vehement suspition, and caried before a Iustice: he handleth the matter in such sort that she confesseth, as I heard of one not long since: her confession was to this effect: She had two spirits, one like a Weasill, the other like a Mouse. These, she said, did manie thinges for her. Now, she accused a woman about ten or twelue miles off, whom (it may be) she did not knowe, and yet could name, and not only that, but said, the woman had, as it were, a litle bigge in her mouth, where the spirite did sucke blood.

Dan. It is a most easie thing for the deuill to tell witches, that such a man or such a woman is a witch, and hath this or that secret marke vpon them. And within these few yeares he hath by witches and cunning men, accused such as were very religious and godly. Men must beware that they proceed not vpō his testimony: he is not to be medled withall, nor any medling which he vseth, is to be taken in good part, seeing he doth all in deep subtilties.

M. B. I do take it, that the testimony of the deuill ought not of it selfe to haue any force with a Iurie, vnlesse it can be proued by some other firme proofes. But what say you vnto this, a witch is condemned, and telleth at the gallows not onlie what she hath done, but also of whom she first had her spirit. She doth this in repentance, and euen readie to depart out of the worlde. It is to bee presumed that she will not in this case lie, nor accuse falsly: Let it be some woman in another towne, whome she saith, brough't her the spirite. This woman is also suspected by some of

her

her neighbours, apprehended and brought to iudgement, and stiflie denieth that she is any witch, or that she euer deliuered any spirite vnto the other which accused her. Nowe here is the question, Is not the testimonie of the woman vpon her death, a sufficient warrant for a Iurie to finde this woman guiltie? here they haue now the testimonie not of the Deuill to proceed by, but of a woman, and though not vpon her oath, yet vpon her death, which is no lesse.

Dan. This testimonie may seeme to be sufficient euen to warrant a Iurie to finde guilty, though it touch life: but if we look well into it, we shall see it is not.

M. B. It may be you take it to be infirme, because it is the testimony but of one.

Dan. Nay, not only in respect that it is the testimony but of one, but that it is the testimony of such a one.

M. B. I put the case of such an one as doeth shew repentance, who though she hath bene bad, yet now may bee beleeued.

Dan. I do not meane in that respect, as to say she was a witch, and therefore not to be credited: but if shee repent neuer so much, yet her testimony in this is weake, because she may be vtterly deceiued, and think she telleth the truth, when it was nothing so, but she vtterly deluded.

M. B. Doe you meane, that he may make the other woman thinke, that such a woman deliuered her the spirit, and neuer no such matter?

Dan. Yea, that is my meaning.

M. B. It is farre beyond my reach to see how that can bee.

Dan. You must consider that the deuil doth many waies delude witches, and make them beleeue things which are nothing so. In Germany and other countries, the deuilles haue so deluded the witches, as to make them beleeue that they raise tempests of lightenings and thunders. For the deuils do know when these things be conming, tempests

of

of winds, and thunders, and faine would he make the blind
world beléeue that those great workes of God, be not Gods
but his : And that is the cause why he coueteth to appeare
in them. These deuils make the witches beléeue, that at
their request they kil both men and beasts, and many waies
afflict, when as many of the things fal out naturally, which
they would séeme to doe, and the rest in which they haue
power giuen to worke, they stirre vp the witch but vnder a
collour for to send them. These deuils make the witches
in some places beléeue, that they are turned into the likenesse of wolues, that they rend and teare sheepe, that they
méet together & banquet, that sometimes they flie or ride
in the ayre, which thinges indéed are nothing so, but they
strongly delude the fantasies of the witches. Euen so the
deuill can delude a poore woman with the likenesse of another woman deliuering a mouse or a catte vnto her, by appearing in such a likenes. Or he can set a strong fantasie in
the mind that is oppressed with melancholie, that such or
such a matter was, which indéed was neuer so. Men must
be wise in these causes, or els may they soon be circumuen-
ted by the craftes of Satan and drawen into great sinne.

*M.* B. If it be thus, then how should a Jurie condemne
by their verdict any witch? For she hath not killed, nor the
deuill at her request, but maketh her beléeue he did it at her
request.

*Dan.* A witch by the word of God ought to die the death
not because she killeth men, for that she cannot (vnlesse it be
those witches which kill by poyson, which eyther they receiue from the deuill, or he teacheth them to make) but because she dealeth with deuils. And so if a Jurie doe finde
proofe that she hath dealt with deuils, they may and ought
to find them guiltie of witchcraft.

*M.* B. If they find them guilty to haue dealt with deuils, and cannot say they haue murdered men, the law doth
not put them to death.

Dan. It wer to be wished, that the law were more perfect in that respect, euen to cut off all such abhominations. These cunning men and women which deale with spirites and charmes seeming to doe good, and draw the people into manifold impieties, with all other which haue familiaritie with deuils, or vse coniurations, ought to bee rooted out, that others might see and feare.

M. B. You will not haue the testimony of Deuils to be of any credit with a Iury, what say you then vnto men, there be some which die, and take it vpon their death, that they are bewitched, and will say precisely such or such haue done it. For that is in the other point touching likelihoods.

Dan. They are bewitched indeed, for the deuill doeth delude their minds: for you shall finde them able to render no reason but onlie this, in their conscience the partie is naught and they are out of doubt it is so.

M. B. That may bee as you say in some, but I haue knowne a woman my selfe which many haue counted to be a witch, and many things haue fallen out where she hath taken displeasure. Do you not thinke that is a firm proofe? She denieth, but the things which fall out, doe manifest her to be naught.

Dan. You must shew the things, and thereby it will appeare.

M. B. She fell out, or els at the least seemed to be displeased with one, and he had an hogge died suddainlie. An other thought she was displeased with him, and his horse fell sicke. A third could not sit vpon his stoole at worke. And within nine or ten yeares space diuers others. One saw the deuill bigger than a cat with great eies. An other was haunted with a spirite. An other brewing, the drinke would not worke in the fatte. An other sawe a thing in her house as big as a lambe, playing in the window: Another in her grieuous torment saw the woman stand by her all the night, whom she suspected to bewitch her, and diuers
such

such like, which were too long to recken vp. If she were not a witch, how should all these fall out so fit?

Dan. I haue shewed already, that where Satan hath a witch to deale by, hee bringeth it about, that in all such things as he hath power giuen him of God, he will seeme to do nothing but requested and sent by the witch. In those things which fall out in sicknesses, lamenes & death, vpon naturall causes, he worketh in such sort, as that he maketh the witch beleeue she doeth them. And this hee coueteth to haue breake forth by her confession. Now, where he hath no witch to deale by, he gaineth exceedingly, if hee can worke in the minds of any a strong suspition of any man or woman. For if it be once begun, hee pursueth it with all his power and cunning. If one bee visited with grieuous torment of sicknes, and be so ignorant, and voide of the faith in Gods prouidence, that he imagine the deuill doeth it at the sending by a witch, the deuill will delude him, and make him beleeue that the witch standeth by him. The man or woman suspected cannot come there: Who then worketh that illusion but Satan? Another is affrayde of the deuill to be sent vnto him, by that partie whome he suspecteth to be a witch: and thus through want of faith in God, giueth the deuill the more power ouer him, either to hurt, or to appeare vnto him. For Satan haunteth all men continuallie, seeking all occasions, and needeth not to be sent by man or woman. They be exceeding blind which will reason thus, an euill spirit came and appeared vnto me, after I had angred such a woman, therfore she sent him. Satan if he haue power to doe harme, or knowe where somewhat will follow, is hee not cunning to make the party which shall receiue the harme, to fall out with some that hee may suspect, and so the harme may seem to come from that partie? Againe, in feare, in the darke men take some litle cat or dog to be an vglie deuill. As not long since a rugged water Spaniell hauing a chaine, came to a mans doore

R 4         that

that had a saut Bytch, and some espied him in the darke, and said it was a thing as big as a colt, and had eyes as great as saucers. Hereupon some came to charge him, and did charge him in the name of the Father, the Sonne and the holy Ghost, to tell what he was. The dogge at the last told them, for he spake in his language, & said, bowgh, and thereby they did know what he was. If he do knowe where harmes do follow vpon naturall causes in men or beasts, he laboureth either to make them offended, and to fall out with the partie that is suspected, or at the least to perswade the of such displeasure conceiued, that the harms may seeme to come from the same. If he do torment indeed hauing power to possesse the bodie, he will not sticke to lie, and to say such a woman sent him.

*M. B.* And doeth it not fall out sometimes, that as he saith such a woman sent him, so the woman vpon examination confesseth so much.

*Dan.* Yea, but I speak where he hath no witch to deale by, but pursueth the innocent with suspition vpon suspition, that men may be guilty of innocent blood. Hee telleth the trueth sometimes, to the end hee may be credited when he doth lie. For let no man be so simple as to thinke, that he will euer tell trueth but for some wicked purpose.

*M. B.* Yet this of all the rest seemeth most strange vnto me, how so many things should fall out, as it seemeth, after the displeasure of a suspected person, and some of them such as apparantly are done by Satan, as in drinke not working, or in creame, when butter will not come, and yet the party suspected is not a witch.

*Dan.* Oh sir the sleights of Satan in compassing such matters be marueilous. I knowe it is taken (as they say) to be dead sure that the party is a witch, if sundry such themes of matters do concurre. But how easie a thing is it for crafty deuils to compasse such matters?

*M. B.* Then you doe not thinke that common fame
is

is sufficient to warrant the conscience of the Iuror, to condemne any.

Dan. Experience doeth teach howe heady much people are in iudging men or women to be witches vpon euerie surmise. And the power imagined to bee in witches,
which breedeth a feare in many, causeth them to bee credu-
lous. Many go so farre, that if they can intice children to
accuse their parents, they thinke it a good worke.

M.B. You say the testimony of the deuill is not to bee
taken, although it be manifest that he doth many times tell
the trueth, because when he speaketh the trueth, hee doeth
it of a bad purpose. And you hold it the testimony of the deuil, not only which he speaketh when anie charge him, but
also which the cunning men & women giue, in as much as
they can say nothing but vpon his word. Moreouer, vnles
I mistake you, the testimony of a witch in many things at
her death, is not as you say any other than the testimonie
of the deuil, because the deuill hath deceiued her, and made
her beleeue things which were nothing so. Besides al this,
you wil haue likelihoods and suspitions to be of no waight,
nor common fame and opinion to mooue the conscience of
a Iurie, because Satan is exceeding subtill in all these.
Then how shall a Iurie finde a witch? What proofes will
you haue?

Dan. Men are vpon their oath to deale, & it doth touch
life, if they doe finde any guiltie of witchcraft. This is a
most waightie matter: whereupon it followeth, that there
must be eyther due proofe by sufficient witnesses, or els the
confession of the witch. For if the testimony be such as may
be false, as al that commeth from deuils is to be suspected:
or if it be but vpon rumors, and likelihoods, in which there
may be exceeding sleights of Satan, as for the most parte
there be: how can that Iury answere before God, which
vpon their oath are not sure, but that so proceeding they
may condemne the innocent, as often it commeth to passe.

L         *M.* B.

M. B. You mistake one point, for the finding of a witch guiltie by a Iury doeth not in all causes touch blood.

Dan. I am not deceiued, for where the Iurie hauing but likelihoods doth find a man or a woman guilty but for killing a beast, it casteth them into prison, setteth them vpon the pillorie, and not only diffameth them for euer, but also if suspition follow again and arraignment, it is death: you see then how neere a way they haue made vnto blood. But if it touch not blood, but the party escape with the imprisonment and pillory, & neuer againe fall into suspition, how grieuous an infamie is it, to haue bene condemned by Iury to be a witch? I speake it where it is only vpon suspition, or such testimonie as is onelie from Satan, and the partie may be cleere.

M. B. It falleth out sometimes that vpon suspition and common fame they hitte right, and the partie which would not confesse any witchery vpon examination, and arraignment, being condemned doth confesse it.

Dan. Let it be graunted that the Iury vpon Satans testimony, or suspitions and common fame, sometimes hitteth right, which yet I feare is very seldome, that is no warrant before God for men that are sworne, for are they sworne to indict vpon likelihoods, or vpon knowledge in that which vpon sound testimony or confession they shall finde? If the party be a witch which is suspected, & yet no proofe, the Iury doeth more rightly in acquitting, than in condemning, for what warrant haue they vpon their oath to goe by gesse, or to find that which they knowe not?

M. B. I doe take it men offend grieuously, if vpon vnsufficient proofe they condemne the innocent, and especially, because they are solemnly sworne: but if they hit right, though it be only by coniectures and likelihoods, I cannot see how they should therein offend: they condemne not the innocent, they do the party no wrong.

Dan. I do not say they are to bee charged with any inno=

nocent blood, o2 w2ong to the partie : but J aske what war=
rant they haue befo2e God vpon oath to touch blood by suf=
pitions. Admit one be arraigned vpon felony, the likeli=
hoods ar great that he is guiltie of the same, but yet it may
be hée is cléere. What is a Jurie nowe to doe? Are they to
venture vpon the life of a man by their oath by suspitions?
Let it be he is one that God knoweth to be guiltie, but no
man can disclose the same, and therefo2e they cleare him,
doe they commit anie offence? Are they bound to find that
which they cannot know? What innocent person then may
not be condemned?

Sam. J p2ay you giue me leaue a litle. J doe not well
conceiue this matter about finding out and condemning of
witches. Jt is somewhat strange vnto me which you speak
J haue my selfe sundzy times bene of the Jurie when wit=
ches haue bene arraigned, we haue found them guilty vp=
on common fame, vpon likelihoods, and vpon such testimo=
nie as you disalow. They haue indéed taken it vpon their
deaths that they were innocent, but that neuer made me to
doubt but that they were witches: fo2 it is saide, the deuill
hath such power ouer them, that he will not suffer them to
confesse.

Dan. What should mooue you to thinke that the deuill
will not haue them to confesse? you sé some doe confesse
when they be examined, and when they be executed : The
deuil hath power ouer the most desperat théues and mur=
therers?

Sam. Yea but he careth not so much though the théues
and the murtherers do confesse, it maketh not so much a=
gainst him, as when witches bew2ay all.

Dan. What, doe you take it he is loath to be diffamed
o2 hardly thought off? Otherwise what should it make a=
gainst him when witches confesse? Jt is some step to re=
pentance when théues and murtherers acknowledge
their sinnes, and if he can hinder them, o2 hold them des=

perate from confessing he will. It is apparant that he coueteth to haue witches to confesse, it maketh so much for
him. He would haue men iudge that there be an hundred
folde moze witches than there be. He disclofeth by his cunning men & women, and otherwise. He coueteth greatly to
haue it thought that he doeth all, in tempestes, in strange
plagues and diseases which light vpon man or beast. And
for this cause hee maketh the witch beleue and confesse
moze than all, that is, that at her request he did that which
he neuer did noz could doe: vnlesse we will denie the soue-
raintie, and prouidence of God ouer all.

Sam, If Satan gaine so much by disclosing them, what
should be the reason that men are generally perswaded, that
he coueteth to haue the thinges kept secret, and so will not
let the witch confesse.

Dan. It ariseth from false perswasions, and fro a false
feare that witches doe so many harmes, and that at their
sending and request the spirites wozke all. If Satan be so
kind and seruiceable to the witch: how is it that he doth not
fetch her some money? For he knoweth where it is lost, oz
where it lyeth in mens houses. He telleth the witch he can
make a man lame. He saith he can kill an hozse. Yea at
sometime he will say he can and will (if she will haue it so)
kill a man. As if it were in his power to doe many great
thinges, and will not but requested. Let vs see if all the deuils can fetch one peny out of a mans house, whose hozse oz
cow they say they haue killed. The coniurer, sayth he, can
coniure him into a man, oz out of a man: let him coniure
him but into a mans chest if he can, to fetch somewhat from
thence. If the deuils can not do these thinges, then be assu-
red that either they make but a shew of killing and laming,
as they do in the most of such harmes, oz else where they do
hurt, it is vpon speciall leaue from God, and not from the
witches pleasure. And to what purpose then should all such
iugglings and shewes serue, if they should be kept close and
                                                                not

# witches and witchcrafts.

not confeſſed.

Sam. Yet for my better ſatiſſaction giue me leaue with＝
out offence to lay open ſome particulars which I haue ſéen.
I was of a Iurie not many yeares paſt, when there was
an old woman arrained for a witch. There came in eight or
ten which gaue euidence againſt her. I doe not remember
euery particular: but the chiefe for ſome thinges were of
ſmall value. One woman came in and teſtified vppon her
oath that her huſband vpon his death bed, tooke it vpon his
death, that he was bewitched, for he pined a long time. And
he ſayde further, he was ſure that woman had bewitched
him. He tooke her to be naught, and thought ſhe was angry
with him, becauſe ſhe would haue borrowed fiue ſhillinges
of him, and he denyed to lend it her. The woman tooke her
oath alſo, that ſhe thought in her conſcience that the old wo＝
man was a witch, and that ſhe killed her huſband. There
came in a man that halted, he tolde a ſhrewde tale. I once,
ſayd he, had both my legges ſound. This old woman and I
fell out and did chide. She ſayd ſhe would be euen with me.
Within thrée daies after I had ſuch a paine in my knée that
I could not ſtand. And euer ſince I go haulting of it, and
now and then féele ſeme paine. There came in an other,
a little fellowe that was very earneſt, me thinkes I ſée him
yet. He tooke his oath directly that ſhe was a witch: I did
once anger her ſayde he, but I did repent me: for I loked
ſomewhat would follow. And the next night, I ſaw the vg＝
lieſt ſight that euer I ſaw: I awaked ſuddainely out of my
ſléepe, and there was me thought a great face, as bigge as
they vſe to ſet vp in the ſigne of the Saracens-head, loked
full in my face. I was ſcarce mine owne man two dayes
after. An other came in, a woman and her child dyed with
gréeuous paine, & ſhe tooke her oath, that in her conſcience
ſhe killed her child. Then followed a man, and he ſayde he
could not tell, but he thought ſhe was once angry with him
becauſe ſhe came to begge a few pot-hearbes, and he denied

L 3                                     her

her: and presently after he heard a thing as he thought to whisper in his eare, thou shalt be bewitched. The next day he had such a paine in his back, that he could not sit vpright: he sayd he sent to a cunning woman, shee tolde he was bewitched, and by a woman that came for pot-hearbes. But she sayd he should recouer of it, and so he sayd he did within some tenne dayes. Then came in two or three graue honest men, which testifies that she was by common fame accounted a witch. We found her giltie, for what could we doe lesse, she was condemned and executed: and vpon the ladder she made her prayer, and tooke it vpon her death shee was innocent and free from all such dealings. Do you thinke we did not well?

*Dan.* Nay what thinke you? Are you sure she was a witch? May it not be she was innocent, and you vpon your oathes shed innocent bloud?

*Sam.* If she were innocent what could we do lesse: we went according to the euidence of such as were sworne, they swore that they in their conscience tooke her to bee a witch, and that she did those thinges.

*Dan.* If other take their oath that in their conscience they thinke so, is that sufficient to warrant men vpon mine oath to say it is so?

*Sam:* Nay, but you see what matters they brought, which perswaded them to thinke so.

*Dan.* Might not both you and they be deceiued in your thinking, or may you vpon matters which may induce you to thinke so, present vppon your oath that you knowe it is so?

*Sam.* If witnesses come in and sweare falsely, the Iurie proceeding according, their testimonie is cleare from blame, for they goe but by testimonie of men sworne.

*Dan.* If witnesses doe sweare directly that in their knowledge a matter was so or so, and sweare falsely, the Iurie is cleare which proceedeth according to their euidence: vnlesse

vnlesse the Iurie do perceiue that their oath can not be true. But what is that to make the testimonie sufficient where men doe but thinke, and can shewe no necessarie reason to ground their thought vpon? As let vs sée in all these which one could proue that she must néedes be a witch. One saith her husband tooke it vpon his death that she killed him, because he would not lend her fiue shillings: doth this proue she bewitched him? Can the deuill kill a man at his pleasure, to gratifie the witch? Is it not rather to be iudged he dyed of some pining sicknesse growing from an euill constitution of body, which the deuill did know, and would set him at some variance with one old woman or other, that so it might bréede suspition of witchcraft.

Sam. You sée there were some things which could not be done but by the deuill.

Dan. In déede the great face which the man thought he saw, was the illusion of the deuill. But is this a good proofe, the deuill appeareth to a man after he hath displeased a woman, therefore she sent him? Doth not Satan haunt all men continually, and would if he could get leaue from God, terrifie them with such illusions? When men are affraide, and haue strong imaginations. What reason did the woman shew which tooke it vpon her conscience that the olde woman killed her child, to proue that it was so? If shee thought so in her conscience, and tenne thousand more with her vpon bare imagination, was that a warrant for you to sweare solemnely that it was so? As for the testimony of the cunning woman that he was bewitched which had the paine in his backe, vpon the deniall of pot-hearbes, it was the testimony but of the deuill, as I shewed before. And what is common fame grounded vpon imaginations?

Sam. Then you thinke we did amisse do you?

Dan. I would not vpon mine oath doe such a thing for to gaine a kingdome.

Sam. It may be she was a witch, although she tooke it

L 4

vpon

# A Dialogue concerning

vpon her death that she was not.

*Dan.* It is rather to be thought she was not a witch: for what should make her deny it vpon her death? The deuill had accused her to be a witch, for direct testimonie against her but his.

*Sam.* You say it was the deuill that told by the cunning woman that she was a witch.

*Dan.* And do you thinke it was any other but Satan?

*Sam.* I did not at that time thinke it was the deuill: but now I see it could be none other.

*Dan.* Then be wiser hereafter, and sorie for that which you haue done.

*Sam.* In déede I haue cause to be gréeued if shee were not a witch.

*Dan.* If she were a witch your warrant was small: but she being no witch, you haue taken away both her life, and couered her with infamie.

*Sam.* I was of an other Iurie since, and there was a woman indicted for a witch, but not for killing any man or child. There came in fiue or sire against her: the first was an old woman, and she sayd she had displeased her, as shee thought, and within two or thrée nights after as she sate by her fire, there was a thing like a toad, or like some little crabbe fish which did créepe vpon the harth, she tooke a beasome & swept it away, and suddainly her bodie was griped. An other fell out with her as she sayd, and her hennes began to die vp, vntil she burnt one henne aliue. A third man came in, and he sayd she was once angry with him, he had a dun cow which was tyed vp in a house, for it was in winter, he feared that some euill would follow, and for his life he could not come in where she was, but he must néedes take vp her tayle and kisse vnder it. Two or thrée other came in & sayd she was by common fame accounted a Witch. We found her giltie, and she was condemned to prison, and to the pillorie, but stoode stiffe in it that she was no witch.

Dan.

Dan. And are you sure she was one?

Sam. I thinke verily shee was one, although there be many of her neighbors which thinke she is none: for how could those thinges followe so vpon her anger? It seemeth they were all done by the deuill.

Dan. He is cunning that can tell that: let it be that it was the deuil which appeared to the old woman like a toad, or like a crabbe fish, and that he did gripe her bodie: doth it follow therefore of necessitie that the other woman sent him? He can not turne him selfe into any likenesse vnlesse God giue him leaue, as he doth in iustice permit that so he may delude ignorāt persons. No witch can giue him power to appeare vnto any in a visible shape. He had this graunted him from God, and Satan by and by will set anger, and then appeare, that it might seeme it grew from that.

Sam. Wee see he appeareth vnto witches, and coniurers.

Dan. Yea but we may not thinke he can at his pleasure take a likenes for to appeare in. That he doth appeare vnto witches and coniurers, it is graunted in Gods wrath to the ende he may strongly delude such wicked people as will not heare and obey the voyce of the Lord God. For the deuils are chained vp by Gods most mightie power & prouidence, and in all thinges so farre as he letteth foorth their chaine, so farre they proceede, one inch further they can not proceede. Where men loue darkenes more then light, hee hath leaue giuen him to do many thinges. Some he terrifieth with vgley shapes, some he intiseth with faire shewes, others he playeth withall in liknes of a Weasell, or Mouse, or some such small vermine.

Sam. I thought Satan could appeare in what likenesse he would, and to whom he would, if the witch sent him.

Dan. Therein you were much deceiued: for the sending by the witch can giue him no power, and if he had power, he would no doubt in all places appeare vnto many as farre

and

and in such sort, as should best serue his turne. Therefore
if he appeare vnto any man, let him thinke God hath giuen
him leaue to goe thus farre with me, and let him call for
faith to resist him, and for true wisedome that he may not
be deceiued nor deluded by him.

Sam. But doth he not appeare sometimes when the
witches send him?

Dan. Where he findeth it is graunted vnto him for to
appeare, he moueth witches to sende him if he haue any to
deale by: but if there be none, yet will he appeare, & deale
so farre as he hath power giuen him.

Sam. But what say you to the womans hennes?

Dan. What should one say to them when they be dead.

Sam. I meane doe you not thinke they were bewitched?

Dan. Christ saith, a Sparrow can not fall without the
will of your heauenly Father: and is not a henne as good
as a Sparrow?

Sam. Nay I am fully perswaded by that which you
haue sayd, that the deuill can not touch any thing to kill or
to hurt it, but vpon speciall leaue from God. They can giue
him no power, she thinketh she setteth him on, and it is he
that setteth her on worke. Let these things be no more called into question: but was it not euident that the deuill killed those hennes? because after the burning of one henne,
the woman had no mo that dyed. If Satan did it not, how
could they cease dying for that? You sayd that he where hee
hath power to hurt in such bodely harmes, is willing to
cease, that such wickednesse may be practised. And then if
this hurt were done by the deuill, is it not to bee thought
that the woman was a witch, seeing it followed after shee
was angry? Let it be that Satan hauing power to do that
he did, would be sent by the witch for a colour, and to make
it euident did set anger betwéen her and that other woman,
to make men thinke that he would not deale, but intreated

by

by her being angry. And so we could doe no lesse but knowe her a witch.

Dan. These be weake foundations to set such a weightie building vpon. For first it is not certaine that the deuill killed those hennes. Might it be they had some infection which he did knowe would kill them, and he craftily bringeth the matter about, maketh two women fall out (which is the easiest matter of an hundreth) euen vpon the dying of the hennes, that so it might séeme they were bewitched. But you say then, how could it be that vpon the burning of an henne, there dyed no more, if the deuill did not kill them? Nay how can you tell but that there should no more haue died, although the liue henne had not béene burned? What if he sawe there should no more die, and thereupon moued the heart of that woman to vse that witchcraft in burning a henne, that it might séeme that was a present remedie to driue away deuils? Or put case he had the power to kill the womans hennes, eyther he is a weake killer, or else he goeth to his worke but lazely. He could kill a great heard of swine quickly when Christ gaue him leaue: could he not if the woman had fiue thousand hennes, haue killed them all at once? Why did the foole then but nibble killing now one and then one, and so was scared away before he had killed all? If he had power before the henne was burnt for to kill why did he not then when they went about to burne an hen kill the rest? It may be he did not knowe what they went about, he was layd soft in his potte of wooll: and comming to kill an other henne, he was mette withall, he smelt the roastmeat, and was scared.

Sam. Then you thinke he did not kill those hennes.

Dan. What certainetie had you that he did kill them? You found it vpon your oath that he killed them, and that such a woman sent him and set him a worke, and yet it is an hundreth to one hee neuer had power for to touch them.

M 2

Sam.

Sam. But what can you say to the other? The man which could not chuse but kisse vnder his cowes tayle?

Dan. I say he was farre in loue with his cow. Let such men learne to know God, & to expell fantasies out of their mindes that the deuill may not haue such power ouer thē, for he worketh in the fantasies of mans mind, and the more strongly where they feare him, as it appeareth this man did. Satan did worke in this mans minde many foolish imaginations, and to make him beléeue he was bewitched he maketh him fall out with one that may be suspected. And thus you Iurie men take your oath & condemne many innocent persons, because you beléeue the deuill, & imagine that witches do that which they can not do.

M.B. I haue heard of many that haue béene condemned for witches which haue taken it vpon their death that they were innocent. And sundry of thē haue had farre weaker proofes brought against them then these that haue bin mentioned.

Dan. Yea that is it which I say, men do so little consider the high soueraignety and prouidence of God ouer all things: they ascribe so much to the power of the deuill and and to the anger of witches, and are in such feare of them, that the least shew that can be made by the sleights of Satan deceiueth them. The only way for men that will eschew the snares & subtilties of the deuil and all harmes by him, is this, euen to heare the voyce of God, to be taught of him by his liuely word which is full of pure light to discouer & expell the darke mistes of Satan in which he leadeth men out of the way. and to be armed with faith to resist him, as the holy Apostle S. Peter willeth, so such as doe forsake this way are reduced into grosse errors & into many abominable sinnes, which carrie men to destruction. I must now bidde you farewell.

M. B. I could be content to heare more in these matters, I sée how fondly I haue erred. But séeing you must
be

be gone, J hope we shall meete here againe at some other time, God keepe you.

_Sam._ J am bound to giue you great thankes. And J pray you when occasion serueth, that you come this way, let vs see you at my house.

_M. B._ J thought there had not beene such subtill practises of the deuil, nor so great sinnes as he leadeth mee into.

_Sam._ Jt is strange to see how many thousands are caried away and deceiued, yea many that are very wise men.

_M. B._ The deuill is too craftie for the wisest, vnlesse they haue the light of Gods word.

_The wife of Sam._ Husband yonder commeth the good wife R.

_Sam._ J would she had come sooner.

_The good wife R._ Ho, who is within, by your leaue.

_The wife of Sam._ J would you had come a litle sooner, here was one euen now that sayd you are a witch.

_The good wife R._ Was there one sayd J am a witch? you do but iest.

_The wife of Sam._ Nay J promise you he was in good earnest.

_The good wife R._ J a Witch? J defie him that sayth it, though he be a Lord. J would all the witches in the land were hanged, and their spirits by them.

_M. B._ Would not you be glad if their spirites were hanged vp with them to haue a gowne furred with some of their skinnes.

_The good wife R._ Out vpon them, there were furre.

_Sam._ Wife why diddest thou say that he sayd the good wife R. is a witch? he did not say so.

_The wife of Sam._ Husband J did marke his wordes well ynough, he sayd she is a witch.

_Sam._ He doth not know her, and how could he say she is a witch?

_The wife of Sam._ What though he did not know her? did he not say she played the witch that hette the spitte red

hotte, and thꝛuſt it into her creame, when the butter would
not come?

Sam. Indeede wife, thou ſayeſt true, he ſaid that was a
thing taught by the deuill, as alſo the burning of an henne
oꝛ of an hogge aliue, and all ſuch like deuiſes.

The good wife k. Is that witchcraſt? Some ſcripture man hath tolde you ſo. Did the deuill teach it? May
the good woman at R. H. taught it my huſband: ſhe doeth
moꝛe good in one yeare than all theſe ſcripture men will
doe ſo long as they liue.

M. B. Who doe you thinke taught it the cunning woman at R. H.

The good wife R. It is a gift which God hath giuen
her, I thinke the holie ſpirite of God doth teach her.

M. B. You doe not thinke then that the deuill doeth
teach her?

The good wife R. How ſhould I thinke that the Deuill doeth teach her? Did you euer heare that the deuill did
teach any good thing?

M. B. Doe you know that was a good thing?

The good wife R. Was it not a good thing to dꝛiue
the euill ſpirit out of my creame?

M. B. Do you thinke the deuill was affraid of your ſpit?

The good wife R. I knowe he was dꝛiuen away, and
we haue bene rid of him euer ſince.

M. B. Can a ſpit hurt him?

The good wife R. It doth hurt him, oꝛ it hurteth the
witch: One of them I am ſure: foꝛ he commeth no moꝛe.
Either ſhe cã get him come no moꝛe, becauſe it hurteth him:
oꝛ els ſhe will let him come no moꝛe, becauſe it hurteth her.

M. B. It is certaine that ſpirites cannot be hurt but
with ſpirituall weapons: therefoꝛe your ſpit cannot ſtraie
noꝛ hurt the deuill. And how can it hurt the witch, you did
not thinke ſhe was in your creame, did you?

The good wife R. Some thinke ſhe is there, & therefoꝛe, when they thꝛuſt in the ſpitte they ſay, If thou beeſt
here

here haue at thine eie.

*M.* B. If she were in your creame, your butter was not very cleanly.

The good wife R. You are merrily disposed *M.* B. I know you are of my minde, though you put these questions to me. For I am sure none hath counselled more to go to the cunning folke than you.

M. B. I was of your minde, but I am not nowe, for I see how foolish I was. I am sorie that euer I offended so grieuously as to counsaill any for to seeke vnto deuils.

The good wife R. Why, *M.* B. who hath schooled you to day? I am sure you were of another mind no longer agone than yesterday.

The wife of *Sam.* Truely goodwife R. I thinke my husband is turned also: here hath bene one reasoning with them three or foure howers.

The good wife R. Is your husband turned to? I wold you might loose all your hens one after an other, and then I would she would set her spirite vpon your duckes and your geese, and leaue you not one aliue. Will you come to defend witches?

*M.* B. We do not defend witches.

The good wife R. Yes, yes, there be too many that take their part, I would they might witch some of them euen into hell, to teach others to defend them. And you M.B. I wold your nagge might hault a little one of these dayes: see whether you would not be glad to seeke helpe.

*M.* B. I would seeke helpe, I would carry him to the smith to search if he were not pricked or graueld.

The good wife R. Tush you laugh, If you were plagued as some are, you wold not make so light account of it.

*M.* B. You thinke the deuill can kill mens cattell, and lame both man and beast at his pleasure: you thinke if the witch intreate him and send him he will go, and if she will not haue him go, he will not meddle. And you thinke when he doth come, you can driue him away with an hoat spitte,

# A Dialogue concerning

or with burning a liue henne or a pigge.

The good wife R. Neuer tell me I thinke so, for you your selfe haue thought so: and let them say what they can all the Scripture men in the world shall neuer perswade me otherwise.

M.B. I do wonder, not so much at your ignorance as at this, that I was euen of the same mind that you are and could not see mine owne folly.

The good wife R. Folly? how wise you are become of a suddaine? I know that their spirits lye lurking, for they foster them: and when any body hath angred them, then they call them forth and send them. And looke what they bid them do, or hire them to do, that shall be done: as when she is angry, the spirite will aske her what shall I do? such a man hath misused me sayth she, go kill his Cow, by and by he goeth & doth it. Go kill such a womans hens, downe go they. And some of them are not content to do these lesser harmes, but they will say, go make such a man lame, kill him, or kill his child. Then are they readie and will do any thing: And I thinke they be happy that can learne to driue them away.

M. B. If I should reason with you out of the worde of God, you should see that all this is false which you say. The deuill can not kill nor hurt any thing no not so much as a poore henne. If he had power who can escape him? Would he tarrie to be sent or intreated by a woman? he is a stirrer vp vnto all harmes and mischiefes.

The good wife R. What tell you me of Gods worde? doth not Gods word say there be witches, and doe not you thinke God doth suffer bad people? Are you a turnecote? Fare you well, I will talke no longer with you.

M.B. She is wilfull in deede. I will leaue you also.

Sam. I thanke you for your good companie.

## FINIS.